Lovestories 4 Girls

Heartbreak Summer

Kirsten Paul

Compact Verlag

Bisher sind in dieser Reihe erschienen:

Band 1: Full Moon Kisses
Band 2: Last Chance for a First Date
Band 3: Flirt But Don't Fall in Love
Band 4: Trouble in Seventh Heaven
Band 5: Heartbreak Summer
Band 6: First Love on a Rainy Day

Weitere Titel sind in Vorbereitung.

Chefredaktion: Dr. Angela Sendlinger
Redaktion: Christina Neiske
Fachredaktion: Monika Bowler
Produktion: Wolfram Friedrich
Illustrationen: Bettina Weisl (MA Illustration)
Typografischer Entwurf: textum GmbH
Umschlaggestaltung: Bettina Weisl (MA Illustration)

ISBN: 978-3-8174-7844-6
7278441

Besuche uns im Internet: www.compactverlag.de

Vorwort

Mit dieser spannenden und romantischen Compact Lovestory kannst du deine Englischkenntnisse spielend leicht verbessern. Eine deutsche Einleitung vor jedem neuen Kapitel hilft dir, den englischen Text zu verstehen. Außerdem werden auf jeder Seite die etwas schwierigeren Wörter erklärt, und durch die Zeichnungen bekommst du eine genauere Vorstellung von den vier Girls und ihren aufregenden Erlebnissen. Blätter doch einfach mal durch!

Jedes Kapitel wird durch Übungen und Tests ergänzt, die richtig spannend und abwechslungsreich sind: Da geht es um Jungs und Liebe, Partys, Freundschaft und Mode – so wird Englisch lernen richtig spannend und cool!

Die Antworten und Lösungen kannst du gleich ins Buch schreiben und hinterher im Lösungsteil nachlesen, ob du alles richtig gemacht hast und was die Tests über dich aussagen. Und wenn du möchtest, kannst du alle Vokabeln im Glossar noch einmal nachschlagen. Slang-Ausdrücke sind mit einem ϟ gekennzeichnet.

Wir wünschen dir viel Spaß mit Nina und ihren Freundinnen – und natürlich viel Erfolg beim Englisch lernen!

Inhalt

1

Summer Time Is Party Time

1

Nina und ihre Freundinnen sind ziemlich aufgeregt, denn die Endjahresprüfungen stehen kurz bevor. Hoffentlich geht alles gut …
Im Anschluss gibt es einen Schulball, auf den sich Nina schon wahnsinnig freut. Natürlich wird sie mit Marcus hingehen, mit dem sie schon seit fast einem Jahr sehr glücklich ist. Doch leider haben Evie, Holly und Emily noch keinen Partner für den Ball gefunden und scheinen auch nicht sonderlich daran interessiert. Da hat Nina eine Idee: Sie will eine Party geben! Die ideale Möglichkeit für ihre Freundinnen, einen Tanzpartner zu finden …

Nina lay on her bed and stared at her yellow bedroom walls. She liked the colour yellow and everything associated with it – flowers, warmth, happiness and summer. She thought back to last summer. She had spent time hanging around with her friends and she had had a great time. Nina had now been in England just a little over a year. At the beginning, she had been a bit sceptical about school and making friends. Now she had a fantastic group

to stare at	anstarren
associated with	zusammenhängend mit
ϟ to hang around	herumhängen

of friends and even an English boyfriend. She looked at the photo of her and Marcus hanging above her desk and admired his cheeky smile. He always made her laugh, even when she was in a bad mood, or if school was really stressful. She couldn't imagine life without him. Suddenly, the phone rang and interrupted her thoughts.

"Hello?"

"Hi, Nina, it's Evie. I was just wondering if you understood what Mr Tillman was talking about in RE today?"

cheeky	frech
RE (religious education)	Religion(sunterricht)
to make a friend for life	eine Freundin fürs Leben gewinnen
to get on well	gut (miteinander) auskommen
Hinduism	Hinduismus
to bring sth. to life	etwas sehr anschaulich erklären
speech	Vortrag

Nina had met Evie on her first day at the new school and within a few days, Nina knew that she had made a friend for life. They were quite different to each other, but got on really well. It was not unusual for Nina and Evie to spend hours on the phone in the evenings, even if they had spent all day together at school.

"Umm... Hinduism, I think," replied Nina. She enjoyed RE lessons and Mr Tillman was very good at bringing world religions to life with his dynamic speeches and dramatic body language.

"I know that..." said Evie. "...but I remember him saying that something was really important for the exams. I just don't remember what."

"I've got no idea," replied Nina.

She didn't know why Evie was asking her about important school work. Usually when they had questions about homework, they would phone their friend Emily. Emily took school very seriously and her parents wouldn't let her go out until she had completed all of her homework.

ÜBUNG 1: Choose the right word! Unterstreiche jeweils die richtige Variante.

1. Nina liked/hated the colour yellow/orange.
2. Nina has been living in England/Germany for a month/year.
3. Marcus was usually unhappy/happy and cheered Nina up/made her angry.
4. Nina and Evie often/never spent time on the phone, because they were close/distant friends.
5. Nina/Evie asked Nina/Evie what they had learnt in the RE/history lesson.

1F

It had been quite a stressful year at school and the end-of-year exams were approaching again. Nina enjoyed school, but sometimes she found it difficult to concentrate during lessons, and she still found the school uniform uncomfortable and unnecessary. She decided to change the subject. "Have you decided yet what you're going to wear at the summer ball?" asked Nina.

"No, I *still* haven't," replied Evie frustrated.
Nina was really excited about the summer ball which the school was arranging to celebrate the end of year. Evie was beginning to get a bit bored of all the talk about dresses, hairstyles and make-up. She was from a large family and much preferred kicking a football around with her three brothers to getting dressed up and going to parties.
"I don't think I'm going to wear my short red dress any more," said Nina.
"But only last week you said that the red dress was the most beautiful thing you'd ever seen," replied a bored Evie.
"It's nice, but it's not suitable for a ball. Why didn't you tell me that it didn't look good for the occasion?! I picked up a catalogue today. It has some gorgeous dresses in it. I think I'm going to get a long blue silk one with a bow and..." said Nina quickly and excitedly.
"Great," interrupted Evie, but she wasn't really listening.
Nina didn't notice and carried on.
"I've got to be prepared so I can tell Marcus what colour bow tie to wear. Wouldn't it just be awful if we clashed?!"

to approach	nahen, bevorstehen, sich nähern
uncomfortable	unbequem
unnecessary	unnötig
to change the subject	das Thema wechseln
suitable	passend
occasion	Gelegenheit
gorgeous	großartig, umwerfend
bow	Schleife
to carry on	fortfahren, weitermachen
bow tie	Fliege
to clash	nicht harmonisieren, sich beißen (Farben)

"Terrible," agreed Evie sarcastically.

"Do you want me to bring the catalogue in tomorrow?" asked Nina.

"If you want," said Evie.

Half an hour passed like this and by the end of the conversation, it was 11 p.m. and time for both of the girls to go to bed. They said their goodbyes and lay on their beds thinking. Nina thought about herself and Marcus dancing at the ball and Evie thought about Hinduism and what might possibly come up at their RE exam. It was only a week away and she didn't feel prepared. There were still three weeks to go until the summer ball, so she didn't yet feel the need to be prepared for that. She wouldn't even go if the choice was up to her, but Nina and her other friends would never let her miss 'the highlight of the year'.

possibly	möglicherweise
to come up	*hier:* drankommen
prepared	vorbereitet
to feel the need	das Bedürfnis haben
(it is) up to sb.	jmd. überlassen sein, von jmd. abhängen

ÜBUNG 2: Synonyms. Finde auf den letzten beiden Seiten im Text die Synonyme der folgenden Wörter!

1. uninterested bored
2. pretty ~~nice~~ gorgeus
3. ironically sarcastically
4. wish want
5. 30 minutes Half an hour
6. go by pass by
7. discussion conversation
8. imagine think
9. test exam
10. decision choice

With all that excitement, Nina couldn't sleep at all that night. She couldn't stop thinking about Marcus and how perfect their relationship was. Consequently, she struggled to get out of bed the next morning and arrived at school five minutes late. This was something that was not tolerated by her form tutor, Mrs Skelton, nick-named by the pupils 'The Owl', because of her owl-like expression and the

consequently	folglich, als Folge
to struggle	Mühe haben
to nickname sb.	jmd. einen Spitz-namen geben
owl-like	eulenhaft
expression	Gesichtsausdruck

way that she wore her glasses on her nose. The Owl took the register and began to talk about careers and the future. Then suddenly she exclaimed:

"NINA!"

"Yeah?" replied Nina.

"Yes what?" responded The Owl, who was obviously getting more and more annoyed.

"Yes, Miss?" said Nina, who still found the English school system very strict compared to that at her previous school in Germany.

"Does this look like a fashion boutique to you?"

"Ermm... No, Miss," replied Nina.

Some boys at the back of the class sniggered.

"First of all, you were late. That was bad enough. And now, you're reading fashion magazines under the desk."

register	Klassenbuch
obviously	offensichtlich
to snigger	kichern
to have eyes in the back of one's head	Augen wie ein Luchs haben
to slide	schieben, gleiten lassen
behaviour	Verhalten, Benehmen
to yawn	gähnen

The Owl certainly had eyes in the back of her head. Nina slid the fashion catalogue back into her bag.

"This behaviour is not acceptable. Especially as you have exams coming up next week," continued The Owl.

"Sorry, Miss," said Nina. She had realized that it was best not to argue.

The bell rang to signal that it was time for the next lesson of the day – English. Nina yawned at the thought of yet more

Shakespeare, but then she thought about how close the summer holidays were.

ϟ to have a crush on sb.	in jmd. verknallt sein
curly	lockig
actually	tatsächlich, eigentlich
poetry	Gedichte, Poesie
confident	selbstsicher
ϟ to talk rubbish	Blödsinn/Müll reden
to join in	sich beteiligen
frilly	aufgeputzt

Holly, a friend of Nina, Evie and Emily's, jumped up from her seat. Normally, Holly wasn't a very active person, but she always looked forward to English lessons. Last year, it was because she had a crush on the young curly-haired teacher, Mr Stubbs, but this year, it was because she actually liked the texts they were studying. In her spare time, she loved reading and writing poetry.

Nina and Holly walked to the classroom together.

"Have you found a partner for the ball yet?" asked Nina excitedly. It was tradition for boys to ask the girls to be their date for the ball.

"I don't think anyone would be interested in going with me," replied Holly, who wasn't very confident because of her weight.

"I feel the same about myself," interrupted Emily, who was walking behind them.

Nina thought that they were talking rubbish.

"Of course they will," she said.

Evie was listening to the conversation, but didn't feel like joining in. She wondered when her friends would realize that there was more to life than silly boys and frilly dresses.

date	*hier:* Begleiter
to raise one's hand	*hier:* aufzeigen, sich melden
inquisitive	wissbegierig
to fail	scheitern, durchfallen
to aim at sth.	es auf etw. anlegen
to gain marks	Punkte bekommen (Leistungsbewertung)
to make a reference to	*hier:* verweisen auf
to relate to	zuordnen, beziehen auf

"I'm going to look huge in my dress," said Holly, who wasn't huge, but a little bit larger than the other girls.
"I'm sure you'll look beautiful," replied Nina and she wasn't lying.
As the girls entered Mr Stubbs' classroom, they finished their conversation, but Nina continued to make plans in her head. She was thinking that it would be brilliant if all of her friends could arrive at the ball together with their dates. She was thinking so hard about this that she almost didn't notice that Mr Stubbs had already started the lesson.
Holly raised her hand: "I have a question about the exam."
"That's marvellous, Holly..." replied Mr Stubbs, "...an inquisitive mind will never fail to succeed." Mr Stubbs always talked in a complex way and aimed at making philosophical comments whenever possible.
"I was wondering if we would gain marks for making a reference to events in Shakespeare's own life and relating them to his plays?" asked Holly.
This question got Mr Stubbs very excited and gave Nina plenty of time to continue to read her magazine under the desk.

ÜBUNG 3: School quiz. Kreuze an, was auf dich zutrifft!

1. What is your favourite subject?
   a) ☒ art, music and languages
   b) ❑ maths and science
   c) ❑ PE (Physical Education)
   d) ❑ I don't like any of them.

2. Do your schoolmates think you are...
   a) ☒ creative?
   b) ❑ serious?
   c) ❑ outgoing and full of energy?
   d) ❑ the joker of the class?

3. What are your plans for the future?
   a) ❑ I hope to get a job where I can express myself.
   b) ☒ I'd like to go to college and then to university.
   c) ❑ I'd love to travel the world.
   d) ❑ I don't make plans.

Five minutes passed and Mr Stubbs was coming to the end of his answer to Holly's question. Nina tuned back in as Mr Stubbs said:

"...and finally, one possibly unique fact about William Shakespeare is that he died on his own birthday." Nina wasn't at all impressed with this statement. She was

to tune back in	*hier:* sich wieder konzentrieren
unique	einzigartig

sure that this was not unique. All she could think about was the ball. She just needed an opportunity to get a date for her friends. Suddenly, she had a wonderful idea. She could throw a party! A summer party. This would be a perfect chance for her friends to meet some nice boys who could take them to the school ball! She would invite all her friends to her house next weekend, after the exams were over. Her parents wouldn't mind. They would probably be out with their friends anyway.

Nina was busy planning her party and choosing her outfit for the ball, but not too busy to plan for German club the next day. She had been running the school's German club for almost a year now and some of the participants had made very good progress. To celebrate the hard work of her club, Nina brought in some traditional German food and drink for the last session of the school year. She brought some sausages, which everybody seemed to enjoy, some German rye bread and pickled cabbage, which were not so popular.

opportunity	Gelegenheit
ϟ to throw a party	eine Party schmeißen
to run a club	*hier:* eine Arbeitsgruppe leiten
participant	Teilnehmer(in)
progress	Fortschritt
session	*hier:* Unterrichtsstunde
rye bread	Roggenbrot
pickled cabbage	Sauerkraut
to mind	etw. dagegen haben
to treat sb. differently	jmd. anders behandeln
by now	inzwischen, mittlerweile
to give sb. a hug	jmd. umarmen

"Urgh, das ist nicht so lecker!" exclaimed Joe, Marcus' best friend, in a perfect German accent.
For the last session, Nina had decided that everybody should try and avoid using English and just speak German. This worked for about 20 minutes, but then everybody went back to English again. Nina didn't mind. She was happy that everybody enjoyed her teaching and that she had made some good friends through the club. She even got to know Marcus through the German club and he also had made very good progress. She tried not to treat Marcus any differently to the other people because she wanted to appear a little like a real teacher.
"You're lucky I didn't bring in some traditional German costumes for you to try on!" joked Nina.
By now it was the end of the session and Nina decided to invite her friends from German club to her party.
"The only thing you'll need to bring is yourselves," said Nina. Everybody started to pack away their things and leave the room. Marcus helped her to pack away the remaining German food and gave her a little hug.

ÜBUNG 4: Short forms. Vervollständige die folgenden Sätze mit der Kurzform!

1. *(I was not)* ... I wasn't .... in trouble.
2. *(She would like)* She'd like to go on holiday.
3. *(They have planned)* they've planned ...... a holiday together.
4. *(You are)* .. You're ..... really lucky!
5. *(They will go)* They'll go .. to Spain.
6. *(I am hoping)* . I'm hoping to see my friends every day.
7. *(I have not seen)* ~~the~~ I haven't seen .... Emily.
8. *(She has been)* . She's been at work. 1F

"I'm proud of you, you'd make a fantastic teacher," he whispered in her ear.

Nina smiled. Suddenly, they both noticed a faint noise in the corner of the room and turned around. They saw Liam, a very shy, skinny boy who was extremely clever.

"The club has finished now, Liam," said Nina.

"I know. I just wanted to tell you that I've had a really good time at German club this year. I even think I'd like to study German at college."

"Oh... well... great... thanks for coming," replied Nina. She was puzzled, because Liam was usually very quiet during her sessions. She had never managed to have a conversation with him before.

faint	leise, schwach
skinny	spindeldürr
college	höhere Schule
puzzled	verwirrt
ϟ party animal	Partylöwe
embarrassed	verlegen
warning glance	warnender Blick
secret admirer	heimlicher Verehrer
to tease	sticheln, sich lustig machen
ϟ geeky brain-box boy	seltsamer Strebertyp

"I'd like to come to your party if that's okay?" asked Liam.

"Liam, the party animal!" joked Marcus.

Liam looked embarrassed and Nina gave Marcus a warning glance.

"Of course. I invited everyone," said Nina.

"Great... well... see you there!" replied Liam before leaving the room.

As soon as Liam had left, Marcus started to laugh.

"I think you've got a secret admirer!" he teased.

"Don't be stupid," replied Nina.

"Geeky brain-box boy loves Nina!" continued Marcus.

"Shut up! I wouldn't want anyone else except you anyway," exclaimed Nina before giving Marcus a quick kiss on the lips. She couldn't wait until the summer when she could spend every day with Marcus, and when no boring schoolwork would get in the way.

Exam week seemed to last for a year. It passed by too slowly, just like it did every year. Emily studied every day and actually found the exams very easy. She answered phone calls from the other girls when they panicked about whichever subject was due the next day. Evie, who was not usually very studious, put in a lot of effort. Nina found the exams quite difficult, but had a good feeling, expecting that she might have passed them all. Unfortunately, Marcus did not have such a positive feeling. After his maths exam, he felt like crying, but of course he didn't. Nina assured him that everything would be alright.

ÜBUNG 5: True or false? Markiere mit richtig ✔ oder falsch – !

1. Marcus didn't like the German session. ☐
2. After the session, everybody left the room. ☐
3. Liam is skinny and clever. ☐
4. Marcus thinks that Liam doesn't like Nina. ☐
5. Nina was looking forward to the summer. ☐
6. Emily studied a lot. ☐
7. Nina found the exams easy. ☐
8. Marcus cried after his maths exam. ☐

to panic about sth.	wegen etw. in Panik geraten
due	fällig
studious	fleißig, lernbegierig
effort	Anstrengung, Einsatz
to assure	versichern
sane	ausgewogen, vernünftig
liberal-minded	tolerant, liberal
high-powered	anspruchsvoll
to make up for sth.	etw. wieder gutmachen, ausgleichen
silky	seidig

The only things which kept Nina sane during exam time were the thoughts about her party, the summer ball and, finally, the summer holidays! On the evening before her history exam, she was busy trying on outfits for her summer party. She decided to wear the red dress, because she thought it was much more suitable for a party than for a ball.

As Nina had expected, her parents were quite happy for her to invite her friends round to their house. They were very liberal-minded and, for many years, had trusted Nina to take her own decisions. They both had high-powered jobs and spent a lot of time and energy on their work. They tried to make up for this by giving Nina money whenever she wanted it. With the money she got from them this time, she bought balloons, decorations and plenty of food and drink. She put the last finishes to her outfit and make-up, brushed her silky blonde hair and waited for her guests to arrive.

"Wow, the house looks amazing and so do you!" exclaimed Holly, the first guest to arrive.

"I just wanted an excuse to wear the red dress I really bought for the ball!" answered Nina.

Marcus and his friends arrived next, all dressed in knee-length flowery surfer shorts and T-shirts. Summer was really here and it was even sunny and warm outside, which was very rare!

knee-length	knielang
flowery	geblümt
inch	Zoll (brit. Längenmaß: 2,54 cm)
to help oneself	sich bedienen
relieved	erleichtert
not everybody's scene	*hier:* nicht jedermanns Sache
to chat	plaudern
edge	Seite, Rand, Ecke
to clear away	abräumen
awkward	unbeholfen

When Nina saw Aimee, a popular girl from school, at the door with a few of her friends, she was a bit worried. She could not remember having invited them. She couldn't even remember how many people she had invited to her party. She had heard about teenagers whose parties had gone wrong and where the police had to be called.

"Come on in," said Marcus to the girls, who were wearing very short skirts and far too much make-up. They often got into trouble at school, as the school's rule was to have skirts no more than one inch above the knee. Nina decided not to let them ruin her evening.

Everyone helped themselves to food and drink and there was a really good atmosphere. Nina had set up a stereo system in the lounge and after an hour or two of eating and drinking, one or two people decided to dance. Evie, Nina and even Holly joined in. The atmosphere was fantastic. Everyone was so relieved that the exams were finally over.

However, this was not everybody's scene. Some of the quieter people chatted in the dining room or stood around the edge of the room, laughing at the people who were dancing. Emily decided to help Nina by clearing away some of the dirty plates and glasses into the kitchen. She was aware that someone was following her into the kitchen and turned around to find an awkward-looking, skinny figure behind her.

"You must be a good friend to help with the clearing up while everyone else is dancing!" said a voice.

"Oh, um, yeah... well, dancing is not really my thing..." said Emily nervously, before realizing that the figure was Liam, whom she had actually never spoken to before.

"Well, I'm the worst dancer ever! To be honest, I don't really like parties or dancing either," said Liam quickly and awkwardly.

"Why are you here if you don't like parties?" asked Emily.

"Funny you should ask that. I only came because I knew you'd be here," said Liam nervously.

Emily started to get worried.

"Um... will... will... will you come... to the ball with me?" stuttered Liam.

Emily was surprised, but thought about the question for a minute. Almost everyone else in the year already

had a date. She didn't. She didn't have anything to lose and Liam didn't seem *that* bad.

"Okay. I look forward to it," she said politely.

She still wasn't sure about Liam. She was a clever and shy girl herself, but liked to think that she also had social skills. Liam, however, didn't seem to know how to talk to girls at all!

Liam awkwardly patted Emily on the shoulder as they walked towards the door. She rolled her eyes and wondered why on earth she had agreed to this!

politely	höflich
social skills	soziale Kompetenzen
to pat sb. on the shoulder	jmd. auf die Schulter klopfen
to moan	jammern, sich beschweren
ϟ Good riddance!	*hier:* Ein Glück, dass wir die los sind!
to drag	ziehen, zerren

As they left the kitchen, they saw Aimee and the other popular girls leave the house. They were moaning about the party and began to talk about the one they would go to next.

"Good riddance!" remarked Nina, as they walked through the door.

"Let's dance!" said Marcus.

He dragged Nina onto the dance floor. They were lost in their own world for a few minutes. Then, Nina glanced over Marcus' shoulder at Holly and Joe, who were also on the dance floor. Joe had his arm round Holly's shoulder.

"Looks like my plan worked," whispered Nina into Marcus' ear.

"Nice one," replied Marcus.

ÜBUNG 6: Reading comprehension. Beantworte die Fragen zum Text!

1. What do Nina's parents do instead of spending time with her?

....

....

2. Which two things did Holly comment on positively when she arrived at the party?

....

....

3. What was the weather like on the day of the party?

....

4. What was Nina's reaction when Aimee and her friends arrived?

....

....

5. Why was Liam at the party?

....

....

6. What did Emily think of Liam?

....

After that they were silent. Above the music, they could hear Joe tell Holly that his uncle owned a limousine hire company, so they could all arrive at the ball together, just like celebrities.

"Fantastic!" said Holly. "I was dreading this ball, but now I'm actually looking forward to it!"

celebrity	Prominente(r)
to dread sth.	jmd. graut vor etw.
to stay the night	über Nacht bleiben
stack	Stapel
waste bin	Mülleimer
ϟ to be sick of sth.	von etw. die Nase voll haben
to cross off	durchstreichen, wegstreichen
hibernation	Winterschlaf

Nina had a great party. Evie stayed the night which meant that neither of the girls got much sleep, because they were talking so much. The next morning, Evie helped Nina to clean up the mess left the night before.

"So, now it's just you without a date for the ball?" asked Nina as she threw a stack of paper plates into the waste bin.

"Hmmm," agreed a very tired Evie.

She was sick of having to agree with her friends to keep them happy. There weren't any boys she even wanted to go to the ball with. She also didn't want to wear a dress. Nina crossed another day off her countdown calendar – only six days to go! Evie felt like going into hibernation for six days, although the one thing that sounded like fun to her was travelling in a limousine. Maybe she could convince Joe to let her ride with them.

2

A Perfect Ball?

2

Der Ball rückt immer näher, und Nina möchte, dass alles perfekt wird! Tagelang feilt sie an ihrem Outfit. Wenigstens hat sie schon ihren perfekten Partner – auch wenn Marcus und sie sich manchmal streiten ...
Am Abend des Balls fahren alle vier Freundinnen gemeinsam mit ihren Begleitern in einer tollen Limousine zur Schule. Alle sind sehr gespannt, und tatsächlich hält der Abend für die vier Mädchen viele Überraschungen bereit! Leider nicht nur im positiven Sinn ...

The next few days passed much more quickly than they did during exam time. Nina dragged Marcus around the shops almost every day as she searched for the perfect bag, shoes and necklace to match her long blue dress. Marcus didn't mind to begin with but after a few days, he wished that Nina would talk about something else. When Marcus was tired of shopping and talking about the ball, she phoned her friends to chat about the preparations for the ball. One afternoon, after a chat with Evie, Nina asked Marcus:
"Why do you think Evie doesn't care about the ball?"

"I don't know. Not everyone likes flowery, sparkly and shiny things. You know that she's a bit of a tomboy." replied Marcus.

necklace	Halskette
to begin with	anfangs
sparkly	funkelnd
shiny	glänzend
a bit of a	ein ziemlicher
tomboy	Wildfang
to burst into tears	in Tränen ausbrechen

"I'm a bit worried about her. I think she's acting strangely," said Nina.

Marcus started to get annoyed.

"Nina, I don't know what's wrong with you. There's more to life than dresses and make-up, you know!" he said in an annoyed tone.

Nina got angry: "Yes, my friends are far more important to me than dresses and that's why I care. You don't seem to care about ANYTHING!"

"I wish you'd just shut up about the whole thing. You're not being at all realistic. You're living in some fantasy world where you're the princess. You need to wake up!" shouted Marcus.

After that, he walked out of Nina's bedroom and out of her house without saying goodbye.

Nina burst into tears. She often had little arguments with Marcus, but they were never about anything serious. She lay on her bed and thought hard about what Marcus had said. It was at times like these that she wished her parents were around for her to chat to. Finally, she realized that Marcus was right. Just because the ball was important to her, it didn't mean that Evie should feel the same. After all,

ϟ like chalk and cheese	verschieden wie Tag und Nacht
to apologize	sich entschuldigen
to wipe	(weg)wischen
mirror	Spiegel

they were total opposites. They were like chalk and cheese.
She immediately phoned Marcus and apologized to him. He accepted the apology and told her that he loved her. Nina wiped the tears from her eyes and tried her hardest not to mention the ball for the next two days.

Finally it was Friday, the night of the ball. The girls spent the afternoon getting ready at their own homes and even the boys spent a little time in front of a mirror. They all met at Joe's house, where his uncle's limo was waiting outside.

Nina had never seen anything like it, apart from on TV and in films. She and Marcus were the first guests to arrive and seemed to be getting along fine after their argument. They had something to drink and some snacks that Joe's mum had kindly prepared, although Nina could hardly eat anything, because she was so nervous. Holly was the next to arrive. She seemed to be in a panic.

ÜBUNG 7: Match-up! Welches Wort kann jeweils auf alle drei Wörter links folgen?

1.	hand, shoulder, plastic	friend
2.	text, story, picture	ball
3.	girl, boy, best	bag
4.	foot, net, summer	book

"I look awful. I just got a huge spot on my chin today," Holly whispered to Nina, as she pointed at a tiny dot on her face. "Don't be silly. You look absolutely stunning," replied Nina. Holly was wearing a long black dress with a green shawl which matched her eyes.
"You look like a superstar," said Joe to Holly completely unprompted. Holly smiled, gave Joe a kiss on the cheek and walked a bit more confidently over to the kitchen to get a drink.

spot	*hier:* Pickel
tiny	winzig
dot	Punkt
stunning	umwerfend
to match	zusammenpassen
unprompted	spontan
suited	mit einem (Herren-) Anzug bekleidet
waistcoat	Weste

The doorbell rang and Joe opened the door to two suited figures. He was surprised until he realized that one of them was Evie. She was dressed in a trouser suit, a waistcoat and she wore a bow tie. She looked very smart.

"Hey guys, you all know Carol, don't you?" asked Evie.
Carol was a small Scottish girl, who had just moved from Glasgow with her family. None of the girls knew her very well, but she was in the hockey team with Evie and they seemed to get on well together.
"I hope you don't mind that Evie invited me. We only decided today. Neither of us had a date and neither of us wanted to wear a dress, so we thought it made sense," said Carol.

ÜBUNG 8: Test – what's your ball style? Kreuze an, was auf dich zutrifft!

1. What would be your ideal dress?
   a) ❑ A pretty black dress with a matching bag.
   b) ❑ Something unique by a famous designer.
   c) ❑ A dress? You must be joking?!

2. How would you ideally get to the ball?
   a) ❑ Any way that didn't make my hair messy.
   b) ❑ In a stretched limousine.
   c) ❑ I'd be happy to walk there.

3. How would you spend your time there?
   a) ❑ Dancing with my friends.
   b) ❑ My date and I would be the centre of attention.
   c) ❑ Chatting at the edge of the room.

She talked so quickly that Joe could hardly understand her. "Don't worry about it. The more, the merrier," said Joe, who was being the perfect host.
Everybody else agreed and started chatting, apart from Nina, who was lost in her own world.

Nina stared into space and thought about how happy she was. She was really excited to be with all of her friends and with her handsome boyfriend at her side. This was going to be the best evening of her life. She thought about the past and how much she had changed during the year she had been living in England. The only thing that hadn't changed were her parents. They were still too busy to spend any time with her and her little sister, which, she thought, was a shame. Then, she began to think about the future. She looked across to Marcus, whose toothpaste smile made her feel warm inside. She couldn't wait to spend more time with him and for their relationship to develop.

ϟ the more, the merrier	je mehr, desto besser
host	Gastgeber
to stare into space	ins Leere starren
handsome	gutaussehend
shame	Schande, Jammer
toothpaste smile	Zahnpastalächeln
to be unlike sb.	ungewöhnlich für jmd. sein, nicht zu jmd. passen

Nina had been deep in thought, but now concentrated again on the conversation, in time to hear Holly say:
"It is unlike Emily to be late."

slightly	etwas, leicht
overweight	übergewichtig
determined	entschlossen
mobile	*hier:* Handy
gravel driveway	Kiesauffahrt
filthy	schmutzig, verdreckt
toddler	Kleinkind
passer-by	Passant

Nina had been so deep in thought that she hadn't even noticed that Emily hadn't arrived yet.
"That's true," agreed Evie.
"The limo is leaving in five minutes!" Joe's uncle shouted out, a slightly overweight man dressed in his chauffeur's outfit.
"I'll phone her to see where she's got to," said Nina, determined not to let anything ruin her perfect evening.
Just as Nina took her mobile out of her handbag, the doorbell rang. It was Liam, who was quite out of breath.
"Sorry we're late, it's my fault," he said.
Emily was struggling to walk down the gravel driveway in her high heels. Nina had never seen Emily in high heels before. She looked gorgeous.
"Why did I agree to this?!" whispered Emily to Nina.
"Come on, he's not that bad," said an optimistic Nina.
"That's okay for you to say. He lost his bow tie at the last minute and I had to polish his shoes for him when I arrived at his house; they were filthy! It's like going to the ball with a toddler!" said Emily. It was not at all like her to complain about anything.
Nina, Marcus, Evie, Carol, Holly, Joe, Emily and Liam all climbed into the limousine and they were driven around the outside of town in style. When some passers-by stared at the car, Nina opened the window and waved as if she

was famous. Emily joined in and wondered what it would be like to be a celebrity who travelled like this all the time. "You look like um... um... that famous actress woman..." stuttered Liam to Emily.

He was desperate to say something which would give him some street cred in front of the others.

"What?" asked Emily.

"The glamorous one with the long brown hair... Angelina Jolie, I think," said Liam, who was gradually becoming more confident around Emily. He hoped that he had remembered the right actress, as he didn't want to embarrass himself any further.

"Well, I guess that makes you my Brad Pitt then," joked Emily.

Liam giggled like a girl and looked out of the window. Nina and Marcus rolled their eyes at each other.

When they were about to arrive at the school, Nina received a text message. She wondered who it might be from, because all of her friends were with her. She was surprised to see that the text was from her mum. For once, she didn't ask her to pick up her sister from school – she simply wished her a good evening. Even though it was a short and simple message, it made Nina really happy. She was grateful to have a loving family, even if they were often busy.

to be desperate to do sth.	verzweifelt versuchen, etw. zu tun
ϟ street cred(ibility)	Glaubwürdigkeit (überzeugendes Auftreten)
gradually	allmählich
to be about to	im Begriff sein zu

ÜBUNG 9: Multiple Choice. Wähle die richtige Fortsetzung zu jedem Satzanfang!

1. It was unlike Emily...
   a) ❑ to be dressed like a toddler.
   b) ❑ to complain about anything.
   c) ❑ to arrive first.

2. Liam was desperate to...
   a) ❑ see the limousine.
   b) ❑ meet Angelina Jolie.
   c) ❑ gain some street cred.

3. He giggled...
   a) ❑ like a toddler.
   b) ❑ like a girl.
   c) ❑ like Brad Pitt.

4. Nina's family was...
   a) ❑ filthy, but happy.
   b) ❑ glamorous, but overweight.
   c) ❑ busy, but loving.

dotted	verstreut
to turn up	auftauchen, erscheinen
stage	Bühne

Inside the hall where the ball took place, everyone had gone to a lot of effort. Groups of friends were dotted around the hall and even some teachers had turned up, all wearing their smartest clothes. There were purple and silver balloons everywhere and the stage was set up for a band. Food and drink was set out on tables at the edge of the room. Nina was really impressed and surprised. Her school in Germany would never have had anything like this. The band came onto the stage and started playing some well-known songs. Nina dragged Marcus onto the dance floor.

"It's amazing, isn't it?" she said.
"Yeah," sighed Marcus.
"You could be a little more enthusiastic," continued Nina.
"I agreed with you, didn't I?" replied Marcus.
"I can't wait to spend the summer with you," said Nina.
"Yeah, it'll be good..."
"I was wondering, you don't have to say yes, if you would you like to come to Germany with me this summer? I was planning to go over there to see my grandparents, family and friends and it'd be soooo good if I could take you with me. I'd love to show them my beautiful boyfriend," said Nina excitedly, as she stroked the side of Marcus' face.
"Okay. I've got nothing else planned anyway," said Marcus.
They continued to dance to 'I'm Walking on Sunshine', without talking to each other. Nina could feel butterflies in her stomach. She felt as if she really was walking on sunshine. She was so excited. So excited, however, that she didn't notice that Marcus' thoughts were elsewhere.

to sigh	seufzen
to stroke	streicheln
butterflies in one's stomach	Schmetterlinge im Bauch
ϟ lad	Junge
ϟ bloke	Typ, Mann

Evie and Carol were having a drink when they were approached by a few lads from their year whom they usually tried to avoid.
"You look like two blokes," sniggered Lee at the two girls.

He was a short but stocky boy, who was usually in trouble for smoking or skiving off school. Evie was used to this kind of comment because of her short hair and the fact that she liked to play football and rugby.
"Why does it matter to you that we're not wearing dresses? Who cares?" retorted Carol in her strong Scottish accent.
"Why don't you speak English?" laughed Sandesh, one of Lee's best friends. This made Lee laugh, too.
It made Evie so furious that she couldn't even speak. Carol was determined to stand up for herself.
"Why don't you just go away and leave us alone?" she said to the boys.
"Your evening is not going to be much fun anyway. Couldn't you get a boy to ask you to the ball? Even that geeky Liam managed to find someone!" said Lee.
"Yeah. You're pathetic," added Sandesh.
Evie knew that they were the ones who were pathetic, but this didn't stop her getting angry. She walked away from the boys and dragged Carol with her. She was so upset that people could make fun of her for not wearing a dress and not having a boy at her arm. She started to think that the whole idea of having a ball at school was completely stupid and nothing more than an over-hyped beauty contest. She told Carol

stocky	stämmig
ϟ to skive off school	blaumachen
to stand up for oneself	sich behaupten
over-hyped	übertrieben, aufgeblasen
beauty contest	Schönheitswettbewerb

that she was going to the toilet, but instead walked towards the door. She needed some fresh air.

As she walked across the dance floor, she almost bumped into Emily, who also seemed to be in a rush to get to the door. Liam called after her: "But..., in the limo..., you... you told me that I was your Brad Pitt... everyone loves Brad Pitt."

"No, Liam, I was joking. I think you got the wrong impression," said Emily as she walked out the door.

"But I thought..." muttered a sad Liam to himself as he stared at the floor.

"I need some fresh air," gasped Evie.

"Tell me about it. Me too!" agreed Emily.

"Lee and Sandesh were really bugging me. They're so annoying. I just had to get away from them."

"What did they do?" asked a concerned Emily.

"They just laughed at my and Carol's outfits, Carol's accent and pretty much everything else they could think of," said Evie.

"At least they didn't try to kiss you," said Emily.

"No way! Liam tried to kiss you?!" exclaimed Evie. This revelation had put a smile back on her face.

to bump into sb.	mit jmd. zusammenstoßen
in a rush	in Eile
to mutter	murmeln
ϟ to bug sb.	*hier:* jmd. nerven
concerned	beunruhigt, betroffen
revelation	Enthüllung

"It was disgusting. He just tried to stick his tongue down my throat without any warning. I had to push him away!" explained Emily.
Evie couldn't help feeling a little bit sorry for Liam because he obviously really liked Emily and had got the wrong idea from her. Emily really had broken his heart.

disgusting	ekelhaft, widerlich
tongue	Zunge
throat	Hals, Rachen
to take one's mind off sth.	nicht mehr an etw. denken, sich ablenken
flustered	nervös, aufgelöst
to dash	rasen
concealer	Abdeckstift
sniffle	Schniefen

The situation had certainly taken Evie's mind off Lee's and Sandesh's awful behaviour. After a few minutes of chatting, the girls were both feeling a lot happier and they were almost ready to go back into the hall.

It was then that a very flustered-looking Holly dashed out of the door. She didn't even wait to be asked what was wrong with her. She simply burst into tears and began her monologue.
"I was so happy that I had a good-looking date for the ball... I should have known that it was too good to be true. I was having a really good time dancing with Joe. Everything was going so well. It is all my fault! If I hadn't cared so much about the ugly spot on my chin, then I wouldn't have gone to the toilets to put some concealer on... when I got back, Joe was dancing with Aimee... I hate her!" Holly said between her sniffles.

ÜBUNG 10: Correct the mistakes. Unterstreiche die acht falsch geschriebenen Wörter und korrigiere sie!

"I need some frasch air," gasped Evie.
"Tell me about it. Me too!" agreed Emily.
"Lee and Sandesh are so anoying. I just had to get away from them."
"What did they do?" asked a concerned Emily.
"They just laffed at my and Carol's outfits," said Evie.
"At liest they didn't try to kiss you," said Emily.
"No way! Liam tried to kiss you?!" exclaimed Evie. This revelation had put a smile back on her face.
"It was disskusting. He just tried to stick his tung down my throat without any woarning. I had to push him away!" expleyned Emily.

1. .... 2. ....

3. .... 4. ....

5. .... 6. ....

7. .... 8. ....

"Well, they were only dancing, it probably didn't mean anything," said Emily encouragingly.
"It wasn't just any kind of dancing... they were really close," sobbed Holly.
"It's funny how life works," said Evie, "while you were having your heart broken, Emily was breaking someone else's heart."

After that, Emily told Holly all about Liam trying to kiss her, which eventually brought a smile to Holly's face. She wiped the tears from her eyes and thought about the situation. It wasn't that bad after all. Joe wasn't the love of her life. She had her best friends with her. The three girls finally agreed to go back into the hall together and decided to stay together for the rest of the evening. They were determined to have a good time, no matter what happened. Just as the girls entered the hall, Nina came over to them.

encouragingly	aufmunternd
to sob	schluchzen
eventually	schließlich, letztendlich

"Girls, have you noticed anything strange about Marcus?" she asked in a worried voice.
None of the girls had really seen much of Nina and Marcus that evening, because they had been busy with their own problems.
"No, why do you ask?" said Evie.
"I just think that he's been behaving a bit strangely," replied Nina.

ÜBUNG 11: Match-up. Verbinde die Gegensatzpaare miteinander!

1.	smart	happy
2.	beautiful	filthy
3.	excited	ugly
4.	lad	casual
5.	laugh	girl
6.	clean	bored
7.	sad	cry

"I'm sure he's fine," Emily reassured her friend. She knew that Nina and Marcus often had little arguments, but sooner or later, they were always back to normal.

"Come on, come and dance the night away and forget about it," said Holly.

to reassure	versichern
bleached blonde	wasserstoffblond
ϟ to hit the dance floor	abtanzen, die Tanzfläche stürmen

She was trying not to look at Joe and Aimee, who looked like a Barbie doll with her bleached blonde hair and far too much make-up on.

"Okay, let's hit the dance floor," agreed Nina, although secretly she couldn't stop thinking about Marcus.

to sway from side to side	sich hin und her wiegen
out of the corner of one's eye	aus dem Augenwinkel
sociable	gesellig
life and soul	*hier:* Mittelpunkt
to nod	nicken

The girls danced like crazy to a few songs and then, when the slow music started, they put their arms around each other and swayed from side to side. Nina kept on looking around the room for her boyfriend. Eventually, she saw him out of the corner of her eye. He was leaning against a wall on his own. This was very unlike him because he was normally a sociable person, who was usually the life and soul of the party. Evie also noticed him.

"I think you should go and talk to him," she suggested.

Nina nodded and went over to Marcus. She was worried that she might have done something to make him annoyed again.

"What's wrong?" she asked, as she put her arm round Marcus' shoulders.

"Don't worry about me. You were just having a great time with your friends," he answered.

ÜBUNG 12: Match-up. Wer sagte was? Verbinde die Satzanfänge mit den richtigen Satzenden!

- ❑ Nina asked the girls if they had...
- ❑ Emily told Nina that she was...
- ❑ Holly suggested that...
- ❑ After noticing Marcus, Evie suggested that...

a) Nina should go and talk to him.
b) the girls should dance and forget about it.
c) noticed anything strange about Marcus.
d) sure that Marcus was fine.

"Come on, spill the beans, Marcus!" insisted Nina.

"Well, seeing you being so happy when you got that text from your parents just made me think. I wish my parents were like yours. Mine are too busy getting at each other to even think about me," he said in a sad tone that Nina had never heard him use before.

"But they are fine, aren't they?" asked Nina.

"They've been arguing for weeks now. They seem to think that I'm deaf, but I've heard every word. Their voices get louder every day. A couple of days ago, I heard my dad say that he had had enough and wanted to get a new life somewhere else."

Nina was shocked that Marcus had been hiding this from her. She knew that Marcus got on really well with his dad. She didn't really know what to say or do, so she just gave him a big hug. Eventually, she said:
"Why haven't you told me about this until now?"
"I don't know. There is absolutely nothing you can do. There is nothing anyone else can do about it," said Marcus pessimistically.
"Well, you should have told me earlier, we could have talked about it," said Nina.
"There's nothing to talk about. *They* can't even talk, they just scream and shout at each other," replied Marcus.

ϟ Spill the beans!	Spuck's aus!
to get at sb.	mit jmd. streiten, jmd. auf die Nerven gehen
deaf	taub
to scream and shout at sb.	*hier:* jmd. anbrüllen, streiten
reluctantly	widerstrebend

"Marcus, it's quite normal for people to argue. We argue, but we still love each other. I've even heard my parents argue a few times. I'm sure it'll be fine, sooner or later," said Nina, although this didn't seem to help Marcus. He looked depressed.
"Don't worry, I'm always here for you," added Nina as she pulled his body against hers.
"Thanks," said Marcus.
"You can talk to me about anything, you know."
"I know," said Marcus reluctantly, as they both started to walk over to where their friends were dancing. However, he didn't seem convinced.

Both Evie and Carol seemed to have forgotten about what had happened earlier and they were dancing as if no-one was watching. Even Holly seemed quite happy, although she had to stop herself looking over at Joe, who seemed to be getting more and more intimate with Aimee. He had totally forgotten about his date. Emily was bopping about happily. Nobody had seen poor Liam since Emily had walked away from him and she assumed that he had gone home.

ϟ to bop about	herumhüpfen
eventful	ereignisreich

For a few more songs, everybody danced as if they didn't have a single worry in the world, but at eleven o'clock the band stopped playing and people started slowly to get ready to leave. The ball had certainly been an eventful evening – one which many of the young people would never forget.

3

A Bad Surprise

3

Zwei Wochen nach dem Ball sind endlich die Prüfungsergebnisse da. Erfreulicherweise haben alle gut abgeschlossen – bis auf Marcus, der leider durchgefallen ist. Nina versucht ihn zu trösten, doch als sich dann herausstellt, dass er nicht mit ihr nach Deutschland fahren darf, ist sie ebenfalls traurig und enttäuscht.
Auf der Rückreise nach England lernt Nina Jonas kennen, mit dem sie sich gleich super versteht. Doch ihre Freude darüber wird von der Sorge um ihre Beziehung zu Marcus getrübt, und als sie ihn schließlich wiedersieht, hat er eine schockierende Nachricht für sie!

After the ball, the girls didn't have much time to see each other. Emily found a summer job in the local bookshop and was delighted about it. When she wasn't serving customers, she spent most of the time with her head in a book to learn about something new. Holly was busy brushing up her Spanish because she planned to go to Madrid with her family. Evie occupied herself by playing sports with her friends and her brothers. Nina was looking forward to her visit to Germany with Marcus. She couldn't wait for him to meet her German

delighted	hocherfreut, begeistert
customer	Kunde
ϟ to brush up	auffrischen
gossip	Klatsch, Tratsch
ϟ to ace sth.	etw. mit links schaffen
to predict sth.	etw. voraussagen, prophezeien
to catch a glimpse of sb.	jmd. flüchtig sehen

family and friends. She knew that they would get along very well.
Just two weeks after the ball, they all met again. They had to go to school to collect their exam results.
There was a lot to talk about and lots of gossip about the night of the ball. Since then, Evie had found out that Sandesh and Lee had got thrown out of the ball for causing trouble, and she was very happy about that. She still hadn't forgiven them for trying to ruin her evening. Emily had received a couple of text messages from Liam, telling her that he was sorry for moving too fast. She had ignored him. The girls chatted enthusiastically while they walked from Evie's house to school. They were all quite nervous because the exams were important and decided which groups they would be in next year.
"Emily is going to ace them as usual," predicted Holly.
"I'm really not sure how I have done. I might pass them all, or I might fail... I just can't wait to find out," said Nina.
However, she was more worried about what Marcus' results would be. He had refused to meet the girls to collect their results, because he wanted to be alone when he collected his. However, when the girls walked towards the school, Nina caught a glimpse of Marcus in front of them.

"Marcus! Marcus!" she called.

He carried on walking as if he hadn't heard her.

"Marcus!" she shouted even louder.

Finally, he turned his head and stood still. Nina could see immediately that he didn't look well. His normally perfect hair looked as if it was out of control and as she got closer to him, she could see that he had big black bags underneath his eyes.

"Are you okay?" asked Nina in a worried voice.

"Yeah, I just couldn't sleep at all last night," answered Marcus.

ÜBUNG 13: Choose the right verb! Unterstreiche jeweils das passende der drei Verben.

1. Emily was lucky to become/find/make a summer job in the bookshop.
2. Holly learnt to pronounce/make/speak 'Te quiero'.
3. Nina knew that Marcus would get off/get along/get out with her German family.
4. Holly prepared/produced/predicted that Emily would do really well in her exams.
5. Marcus rejected/received/refused to meet the girls to get their exam results.

"Come on, let's go in. We'll be celebrating soon," said Nina optimistically as she linked arms with Marcus. She didn't think it was the right time to ask about his parents or the reasons why he had not slept last night.

As the girls entered the hall, they saw The Owl, who immediately took Emily to one side. She looked delighted.

"This is the first time someone in my form has won the award for the best results in their year. Congratulations, you did brilliantly!" exclaimed The Owl.

Nina, Evie and Holly took their envelopes from the table and opened them at the same time. They all shrieked with delight and hugged each other when they realized that they had passed their exams in all of the subjects. Emily came over to join them and they all celebrated together.

For a moment, Nina was so happy that she forgot about her boyfriend. When she turned around, she saw Marcus as he left the room, the envelope clenched in his fist. Nina followed him.

"There's no use in running away," said Nina.

black bags underneath one's eyes	dunkle Ringe unter den Augen
to link arms with sb.	jmd. unterhaken
form	Klasse
envelope	Umschlag
to shriek with delight	vor Freude schreien, kreischen
to hug	umarmen
to clench sth.	etw. umklammern, festhalten

miserably	unglücklich
failure	Versager, Misserfolg
to retake exams	Prüfungen/ Klassenarbeiten wiederholen
talkative	gesprächig
to ground sb.	jmd. Hausarrest erteilen
to be due to do sth.	etw. tun sollen

"Well, I feel like running away," said Marcus miserably. He looked as if he was about to cry.

"I've got nothing to stay here for. I'm a complete failure. My family is failing, I've failed my exams..." he continued.

Nina was shocked. She was not so surprised that he had failed his exams, but she had never heard Marcus talk like this before. He was normally such a positive person. Once again she found herself hugging him and reassuring him that everything would be okay. It took Nina a few more minutes before she found out that he had failed the exams in most of his subjects. Therefore, he was getting worried about having to retake the failed exams.

"At least we've got our little holiday to look forward to," said Nina. Then she invited him over to her house, but Marcus refused and insisted on going back home on his own.

A few hours later, Nina phoned Marcus to see if he was any better. He wasn't very talkative and seemed even more upset than earlier. He told Nina that he had been arguing with his mum. His mother was annoyed with his bad exam results and had grounded him for two weeks. This also meant that he was not allowed to go to Germany with Nina, because they were due to leave in two days.

ÜBUNG 14: Unscramble the sentences! Bringe die Satzteile in die richtige Reihenfolge.

1. sleep at all – I just couldn't – last night

....

....

2. has won the award – someone in my form – this is the first time – for the best results in their year

....

....

3. use in – there's no – running away

....

4. I'm a – stay here for – I've got – complete failure – nothing to

....

....

5. at least – our little holiday – to look – we've got – forward to

....

....

Again Nina tried her hardest to reassure Marcus, but as she finally hung up the phone, she was completely devastated. She lay on her bed for a few minutes. She should have been so happy. She had just got really good marks in her exams. She should have been looking forward to going to Germany, but now she wasn't. It was time to call her friend Evie. She was always good at cheering her up.

"Hi, clever clogs," said Evie.

"You too," replied Nina. "I am so upset, Evie. I don't know what to do. I should be so happy, but Marcus has made me feel really down. He's failed most of his exams, he's got family problems, and now he's not allowed to come to Germany with me! I'll have to go and see my family on my own," said Nina.

to hang up	auflegen
devastated	am Boden zerstört
mark	(Schul-)Note
ϟ clever clogs	Schlaukopf
selfish	egoistisch
to doubt sth.	etw. bezweifeln
at such short notice	so kurzfristig
resort	Ferienort

"Uhuh," said Evie, indicating that she was listening and that Nina should continue.

"I feel so selfish. Obviously Marcus has problems, but he has ruined my summer, too. I can't go on holiday on my own!" said Nina.

"Well, it's not the end of the world. You could, maybe, convince his parents to let him come," said Evie.

"I really doubt it. I'd be scared to even talk to his parents. They have their own problems, and at the moment, Marcus has no choice but to respect their decision."

"Well, maybe, you could take someone else instead," suggested Evie.

"At such short notice? It's the day after tomorrow!" exclaimed Nina.

Suddenly, something clicked in Nina's mind. A holiday with one of her best friends would almost be as good as a holiday with her boyfriend!

"You're not going away until later in the holiday, are you?" she asked.

"Yeah, and even then I'm only going to yet another boring English seaside resort with my parents. So, until then, I'm staying at home," replied Evie.

"What do you think about spending a week in Germany?"

Evie was excited at the idea of going away with Nina.

"Yes! Yes! I'd love to!" she exclaimed.

She had never been away from home before with a friend for a whole week. She was sure that her parents would say yes. If they had any doubts, she could convince them that she was going there to practise her German.

The girls started to discuss what they would pack and what they would do when they got there.

Two days later, Evie's brother Olly drove his sister and Nina to the airport. Evie was excited because she had never been to Germany before. She didn't really know what to expect.

ÜBUNG 15: Unscramble the words. Ordne die Buchstaben zu sinnvollen Wörtern!

1. Nina tried her hardest to (sarserue) .... Marcus.
2. She is leaving the day after (rrmtwooo) ....
3. It clicked in Nina's (dinm) ....
4. Marcus has to respect his parents' (iioscend) ....
5. Liam wants to be Emily's (benoyfird) ....
6. The summer (lohayids) .... are here!
7. Evie is going on holiday with her (rapesnt) ....
8. (sngtayi) .... at home would be boring.

Nina was also excited about seeing her family and friends again. However, as they were boarding the plane, she secretly wished that Marcus was there with her instead of Evie. She had said goodbye to Marcus the night before and had done her best to cheer him up. Now she was determined to try and put the thoughts about her boyfriend to one side and to enjoy her holiday.

Nina's aunt Dagmar and her uncle Lukas picked the girls up from the airport and took them to their home where they where going to stay. They had a great week with Nina's family and friends and Evie was very enthusiastic about Germany. Nina was happy to show her everything and to introduce her to her German friends. The girls really enjoyed their holiday very much.

The only thing Nina was nervous about was her relationship with Marcus. She texted him every day, but his answers were rather short and cold. Nina found this very strange, because Marcus nearly always added kisses at the end of his messages. He hadn't added a single one, despite the fact that she always added them to her

to board	einsteigen, an Bord gehen
secretly	insgeheim
to pick sb. up	jmd. abholen
to text sb.	jmd. eine SMS senden
rather	ziemlich
despite	trotz

messages. She tried to convince herself that it must be because he was stuck in the house with his parents and was probably a bit jealous that she was on holiday without him. But deep inside, she couldn't help but think that something was seriously wrong.

The week seemed to fly by for both the girls. All of the activities they crammed in didn't give Nina too much time to think about Marcus. Before they knew it, it was time to say goodbye to Dagmar and Lukas.

When they arrived at the airport, both the girls were really tired from their active days and late nights, spent listening to Lukas' stories. Nina closed her eyes, relaxed and listened to her MP3 player, while Evie flicked through a guidebook about a castle they had visited on her first day in Germany. However, she didn't find it quite so interesting now, because the stories didn't seem as real as when she had been there. She began to use her imagination to picture the castle in the distant past.

to be stuck	festsitzen
jealous	eifersüchtig
to fly by	verfliegen, im Flug vergehen
to cram in	hineinpacken
to flick through	durchblättern, überfliegen

"Fantastic place, isn't it?" she heard a voice say.

She looked up and saw a tall blonde boy sitting opposite her.

"Yeah, it was amazing," agreed Evie.

"I've been there loads of times... my dad is German, and I've got a lot of family in the area... my name is Jonas, by the way."

"Hi, I'm Evie. Nice to meet you," she said as he shook her hand firmly.

They started to chat about the differences between Germany and England and got on really well.

scenery	Landschaft
to rub	reiben
dimples	Grübchen

"I really think I could live in Germany. The history, the food, the scenery... but I'd have to bring Nina along, so that she could translate!" said Evie to Jonas.

At the mention of her name, Nina opened her eyes and stretched her arms above her head.

"You were lost on a different planet... a musical planet maybe?" joked Jonas.

"Oh, erm, I was half asleep," admitted Nina as she rubbed her eyes. Who are you?"

"Jonas," he said, smiling.

"Why are you talking about me?" asked Nina, still stretching.

"So, you must be Nina then?" said Jonas.

He had dimples in his cheeks which got bigger when he smiled. Something he obviously did quite often.

"Oh, sorry... yes, I'm Nina."

"Don't worry. Nice to meet you both, it's definitely better than waiting around on my own," said Jonas.

The conversation continued and after about fifteen minutes, both the girls felt as if they had known Jonas for years. They found out that he was sixteen, had lived in Germany until he was eleven and then moved to England to start secondary

departures board	*hier:* Abflugtafel
like-minded	gleichgesinnt, auf gleicher Wellenlänge
to lend	leihen
well-thumbed	zerlesen

school. Evie went to check the departures board and Nina continued to chat with Jonas. She found out that they both liked the same books and the same bands. She didn't usually talk to strangers, but they got on brilliantly, so she was glad that he had started the conversation with Evie. Nina was happy to have found someone like-minded.

Evie returned and told them they had to go to the departure gate. Nina and Evie took out their boarding cards and realized that they weren't sitting all next to each other on the plane. Unfortunately, Jonas was sitting at the front and they were sitting at the back.

"I can lend you a magazine to pass the time if you want," offered Jonas. "I need lots of reading material when I'm

staying with my grandparents. It's not the most exciting way to spend a holiday."
He handed her a well-thumbed music magazine.
"Yeah, that'd be fantastic," Nina said.

ÜBUNG 16: Who said what? Antworte immer mit einem ganzen Satz!

1. Who said that he/she had been to the castle many times before?

....

2. Who said that he/she could imagine living in Germany?

....

3. Who told Nina that she looked as if she was on a different planet?

....

4. Whose excuse for not listening was that he/she was sleepy?

....

5. Who told the others that it was time for the flight?

....

6. Who offered to lend Nina a magazine?

....

The flight passed quite quickly and before they knew it, they landed in rainy England. Nina switched on her phone and checked her voicemails. There was a message from Marcus, telling her that he needed to talk to her as soon as possible and that he would be waiting for her at his house. His voice sounded so cold and distant that Nina immediately became nervous.

She almost missed her suitcase coming around on the carousel, because she was so caught up in her thoughts. She grabbed her case and turned towards passport control, where she saw the back of a tall blonde boy with his big rucksack walking out of the luggage area. Jonas! In all the chaos she hadn't realized that she still had his magazine. She hoped that he didn't want it back. For a moment, she wished that she had had the courage to ask for Jonas' phone number. Nina had never before met a boy she got on so well with so quickly...

Suddenly, reality hit her. She couldn't believe that she was thinking about an almost complete stranger, when she didn't even know what was happening to her relationship with Marcus.

voicemail	Nachricht auf dem Anruf-beantworter
carousel	*hier:* Gepäck-band
caught up in one's thoughts	in Gedanken vertieft
luggage area	Gepäckbereich, Gepäckabholung
to be hit by reality	von der Realität eingeholt werden
to drop sth.	etw. fallen lassen

***ÜBUNG 17:** Hidden words. Finde im Suchrätsel 11 Wörter, die Beziehungen betreffen!*

argument *date* *fancy* *crush* *kiss* *love*

girlfriend *hug* *dump* *cheat* *boyfriend*

B	S	A	P	Y	E	A	H	U	G
A	O	C	O	H	O	P	M	S	I
R	K	Y	P	S	D	U	M	P	R
G	E	C	F	U	G	L	H	O	L
U	G	N	L	R	K	O	P	G	F
M	A	A	S	C	I	V	J	A	R
E	E	F	B	I	S	E	S	L	I
N	T	I	N	E	S	J	N	S	E
T	A	E	H	C	T	I	O	D	N
M	D	U	Q	X	B	D	G	F	D

As soon as Nina arrived at home, she dropped her heavy suitcase at the bottom of the stairs, quickly said hello to her family and then walked straight to Marcus' house. She couldn't wait to see him to find out what was wrong with him.

He invited her in and they went straight up to his bedroom. They talked about the last week, but then Nina asked him to tell her what was going on, what was upsetting him so much.

Marcus looked at her in silence, then he burst out: "My parents are getting divorced. They're selling this place and they are going to move away." He said this without any real emotion in his voice.

Nina was shocked. She couldn't believe that her boyfriend was moving away.

"My mum is moving to London and my dad has a new job in Newcastle and I'm going to go with him," explained Marcus.

"But... but... that's not fair! How do you feel? Aren't you upset?" asked Nina nervously.

"I think it's a good opportunity... I was gutted to begin with, but I think I need a new start... maybe I'll find some new friends and maybe even get better exam results... after the retakes," said Marcus.

Nina was surprised at the lack of emotion in his voice.

"But, Nina..." he continued.

"Oh, don't worry, I'm sure I could get there by train... I could visit you every couple of weeks and you could..." said Nina as she tried to put her arm around Marcus, who immediately pulled away from her.

"Nina, you're not listening... I just don't think I can deal with a long-distance relationship. Umm, I mean, it's not you... I'm just too young for that. I think a completely fresh start would be good for me. I mean, a *completely* fresh start..."

It took Nina a minute or so to understand what she had just heard.

to get divorced	sich scheiden lassen
place	*hier:* Haus, Wohnung
ϟ gutted	am Boden zerstört
retakes	Nachprüfungen
lack of	Mangel an
to pull away from sb.	sich jmd. entziehen, ausweichen
to deal with sth.	mit etw. klarkommen
long-distance relationship	Fernbeziehung
ϟ to dump sb.	mit jmd. Schluss machen
speechless	sprachlos
mood	Stimmung

"So... so... you're dumping me?" she asked. She couldn't believe what she had just heard. The whole situation didn't seem real to her. It felt as if this was all a bad dream.

"Nina, I've had a really good time with you, but as I said, I just don't think we can continue to go out together... I'm moving next week..." Marcus said while he stared into a corner of his room.

After that comment, Nina was speechless. She couldn't even cry. All she could do was to walk out of Marcus' room and out of his house. She thought about the fact that she might never see him again and she was devastated. She walked down the streets she knew so well, but they didn't seem the same now. The orange sun was setting behind the trees along Marcus' street but Nina was too busy to notice, she was staring at the ground. The familiar walk seemed to take ten times longer than it had taken to reach his house. As soon as she returned home, she went straight to her bedroom. She was not in the mood to talk to anyone.

occasionally	gelegentlich
to blow one's nose	sich die Nase putzen

Nina spent most of the following day sitting in her room on her own, thinking about Marcus. She didn't leave her bedroom, apart from occasionally getting some crisps, a drink and chocolate from the kitchen. How could he do this to her? He had told her that it wasn't because of her. But surely, if he loved her, he would at least try a long-distance relationship. Newcastle wasn't *that* far away. Maybe it was just an excuse. Maybe it was her fault. Maybe she hadn't listened to him enough. She had never given him the chance to talk about how he felt. She should have realized this earlier. These kinds of thoughts went round and round in her mind for hours and hours. Sometimes, she burst into tears and just let them fall onto her pillow. She didn't even blow her nose. For the whole day, she just sat on her bed in her pyjamas.

ÜBUNG 18: Multiple Choice. Wähle die richtige Fortsetzung zu jedem Satzanfang!

1. Nina and Marcus talked in...
   a) ❑ a coffee shop.
   b) ❑ Marcus' room.
   c) ❑ Nina's room.

2. Marcus is moving to...
   a) ❑ Manchester.
   b) ❑ London.
   c) ❑ Newcastle.

3. When he told Nina that he was moving, Marcus' voice was...
   a) ❑ angry.
   b) ❑ emotionless.
   c) ❑ upset.

4. When he split up with Nina, she said...
   a) ❑ nothing.
   b) ❑ that she wouldn't let him give her up.
   c) ❑ that she didn't like him anyway.

5. Nina didn't...
   a) ❑ cry.
   b) ❑ think about what had happened.
   c) ❑ blow her nose.

Her parents knew that something must have happened between her and Marcus. Her mum told her that she was there for her if she wanted to talk, but left Nina alone in her room.

to be in touch	in Verbindung sein, sich melden
mess	Chaos

At about six o'clock in the evening, Nina's mum shouted up the stairs to tell her that she had a visitor. It was Evie, who was worried that something may not be right with Nina, because she hadn't been in touch all day. They would usually exchange text messages, phone each other or meet to do something together.

Nina wasn't in the mood to see anyone at all, but she slowly walked down the stairs and heard Evie chatting to her mum about their holiday in Germany. She was telling her mum about how great her sister Dagmar was. Nina really wasn't in the mood, but couldn't exactly send her friend home.

"Do you want to come up to my room?" asked Nina without even looking at her mum.

Evie followed her friend up the stairs. Nina's usually perfect room was in a complete mess, with clothes and other items all over the floor. She hadn't been in the mood to tidy it up or to unpack from her holiday.

Evie looked at Nina's red eyes and knew immediately that something had happened between her and Marcus:

"So, start at the beginning and tell me everything!"

4

Heartbreak and Suspicions

4

Nachdem Nina ihrer Freundin das Herz ausgeschüttet hat, geht es ihr schon viel besser. Schließlich überwindet sie sich sogar, wie ursprünglich geplant mit Evie, Holly und Emily zur Rollschuhdisco zu gehen.
Dort kommt Nina allerdings ein schrecklicher Verdacht: Kann es wirklich sein, dass Marcus sie mit der hübschen Aimee betrogen hat und deshalb mit ihr Schluss gemacht hat?
Am nächsten Tag versuchen ihre Freundinnen, sie zu einem Anruf bei Jonas zu überreden. Doch Nina zögert – ist es dafür nicht noch zu früh?

Nina felt much better after telling her friend what had happened. As always, Evie was sympathetic and good at listening as Nina poured her heart out. Evie tried to reassure her:

"I'm sure he was really upset, too... He was probably confused about moving and just didn't know what to do... I know that he really likes you," said Evie.

"Well, I wouldn't say that he was that upset. He wouldn't even look at me!" said Nina.

"Well, that shows that he feels bad," said Evie reassuringly. She somehow knew what to say, probably because she had seen her older brothers break up with so many girlfriends!

sympathetic	mitfühlend
to pour one's heart out	sein Herz ausschütten
to break up with sb.	mit jmd. Schluss machen
grumpily	mürrisch

"He obviously doesn't feel too bad to meet Joe and some of the others," sobbed Nina.
"Which others?" asked Evie. She was sure that Joe had told her that all his friends were on holiday.
"Well, he wasn't very specific," replied Nina. She was so upset that Marcus could just dump her and continue having fun, while she was lying on her bed in her pyjamas crying.
Evie didn't know what to say about the whole story. For a minute or so, the girls did not speak at all.
"I know that this is a really bad time to ask, but are you still coming to the roller disco this evening?" Evie asked eventually, breaking the silence. "I'm going to have to go soon, because I'm meeting Emily before we go over there."
Nina had completely forgotten that she had agreed to go to the roller disco. It had been arranged weeks ago and Nina had been looking forward to it. Now, she couldn't think of anything else she would like to do less.
"No. I'm really not in the mood for dancing and having fun," Nina said grumpily.

"It might do you some good to get out of the house for a while," replied Evie.

"Everyone would ask me where Marcus was and I really don't want to talk about him having dumped me, or talk about him at all!" said Nina.

"Well, you're going to have to face it sooner or later," said Evie.

"I think I'm just going to get an early night if you don't mind. I'm sorry. I know, I promised that I would come, but things have changed," said Nina.

"Of course..."

Evie could understand why Nina didn't want to go to the roller disco, so she told her that she would come and see her again the next day.

"Hmm, if you want," said Nina. She just felt like curling up into a ball on her bed.

"Of course I want to, silly... We'll miss you tonight," said Evie.

"I know... thanks for everything," said Nina as she hugged her friend. Sometimes, she didn't know what she would do without her.

to face sth.	sich einer Sache stellen
to get an early night	früh zu Bett gehen
to feel like doing sth.	Lust haben, etw. zu tun
to curl up into a ball	sich zusammen-rollen, sich einigeln
to pull oneself together	sich zusammen-reißen
to miss out on sth.	etw. verpassen, sich etw. entgehen lassen
sore	gereizt

ÜBUNG 19: Odd one out. Welches Wort ist das „schwarze Schaf“?

1. upset, annoyed, delighted, angry
2. brother, cousin, aunt, neighbour
3. jeans, pyjamas, skirt, slippers
4. quiet, noisy, calm, silent
5. cry, sob, moan, break
6. hug, push, kiss, stroke

After Evie had left, every minute that passed seemed to last an hour to Nina. She was so bored of being lonely in her room. She stared at herself in the mirror and said in a loud voice:
"Nina, pull yourself together!"
Then she walked to the bathroom, washed her face and brushed her hair for the first time since she had been in Dagmar and Lukas' bathroom in Germany. She put on her favourite denim skirt and a blue vest-top and went downstairs to ask her mum for a lift to the disco. It would have taken too long to walk because the disco had already started an hour ago. She didn't want to miss out on any of the fun. Her eyes felt sore, but she was determined to have a good time. She was looking forward to seeing

Holly, Emily and some other friends, whom she hadn't seen for a couple of weeks. She was glad that Evie had come over to see her, otherwise she would have completely forgotten about the roller disco.

factory	Fabrik
derelict	baufällig, herrenlos
to blare out	herausschmettern
intriguing	faszinierend
disused	ausgedient, stillgelegt
You scared the life out of me!	Du hast mich zu Tode erschreckt!
to mope around the house	zu Hause sitzen und Trübsal blasen

The disco was held outdoors, in a large open space next to the railway line on the edge of town. The area used to be the industrial centre of the town because it was where the factories were located. Now, most of the buildings were derelict. It was a really warm summer's evening. The music was blaring out and there were no neighbours to complain. Nina had always liked this part of town. She found it intriguing. She got out of the car and stared up at the chimneys of the disused factories.

"Boo," said a voice, and Nina felt someone run into her back.

"Aaagh!" Nina exclaimed as she turned round to see Evie, who had skated into the back of her.

"You scared the life out of me!" exclaimed Nina.

"I was just surprised to see you here," said Evie, "but of course, I'm happy!"

"I was a bit bored of moping around the house," said Nina.

"Well, let's go and hire you some skates and we'll go to find the others," said Evie excitedly.

She skated off energetically and Nina struggled to follow her through the crowds. She was surprised at how many people were there, but then a thought occurred to her.

"Evie..." she shouted.

Evie spun around briskly and skated back towards Nina.

"No, he's not here," said Evie, before Nina could even ask the question. This made Nina laugh.

"I can't believe that you are also a mind-reader!" giggled Nina. She was lucky to have such a good friend.

Nina hired her skates and shakily followed Evie over to the edge of the rink, where a group of her friends were having a rest. Joe and Emily were standing up; beside them stood Liam, who was doing his best not to overbalance on his skates and fall over. Nina was surprised to see him there after what had happened at the ball. Holly was sitting on the concrete floor sipping a lemonade. She was a bit sunburnt from her holiday in Spain and looked absolutely exhausted.

to hire	mieten
to occur to sb.	jmd. in den Sinn kommen
to spin around	herumwirbeln
briskly	flott, rasch, zügig
mind-reader	Gedankenleserin
shakily	wackelig
rink	*hier:* Rollschuhbahn
concrete floor	Betonboden
exhausted	ausgepowert, erschöpft

ÜBUNG 20: Adjective forms. Setze die fehlenden Formen ein. Achtung: Einige sind unregelmäßig!

bored	1.	most bored
good	better	2. ....
large	3.	4. ....
warm	warmer	5. ....
6.	7.	most surprised
determined	8.	9. ....
friendly	10.	friendliest

"Hi, everyone," Nina greeted her friends.
They all said their hellos, but no-one started a conversation with her. Nina felt awkward and realized that Evie must have told them about her and Marcus, so nobody quite knew what to say to her.
"Anybody wants to do a few laps?" shouted Nina over the loud music.
Everybody, apart from Holly, agreed and set off.
Nina skated alongside Emily.
"I'm surprised your parents let you come to this part of town," commented Nina.

Emily's parents were so strict that they often wouldn't even let her go shopping in the town centre.
"Well, they don't really know where I am. I told them I would go to the cinema," said Emily as they began to get into the swing of things and skated even faster.
"Good for you!" exclaimed Nina, who often wished that Emily would be more daring and would rebel a little bit.
"And what's going on with that Liam guy?" asked Nina.
At that moment, Liam skated shakily over to them, so Emily had no chance to answer. After a few more laps, Nina started to get tired, so she went over and joined Holly, who was looking slightly less red.
"Tiring, isn't it?" asked Nina.
"Yeah. I'm sorry to hear about you and Marcus," replied Holly.
Nina knew that Holly really was sorry. Holly was a romantic dreamer and hated it when relationships went wrong. However, Nina did not want to talk about him.
"Yeah, well, these things happen," replied Nina, trying to hold back her tears.
Holly noticed that Nina was upset and decided to change the subject.
"Come on, let's go and get something to eat," said Holly and pointed towards the hotdog stall.

lap	*hier:* Runde
to get into the swing of things	in Schwung kommen, sich auf etw. einlassen
daring	mutig, waghalsig
stall	Stand

Nina realized that she had hardly eaten anything during the past three days and was glad of the offer.

ÜBUNG 21: Test: Are you a good girl? Kreuze an, was auf dich zutrifft!

1. You find £50 in a wallet on the street, do you...
   a) ❑ take the cash? *(5 points)*
   b) ❑ phone the owner, hoping he or she will give you a reward? *(3 points)*
   c) ❑ take it straight to a police station? *(1 point)*

2. Your teacher leaves a copy of the next maths exam on his desk and you find it. Do you...
   a) ❑ copy it? *(5 points)*
   b) ❑ have a quick look at it? *(3 points)*
   c) ❑ return it to the teacher? *(1 point)*

3. Your parents go out for the evening and tell you not to have friends over, do you...
   a) ❑ watch a DVD on your own? *(1 point)*
   b) ❑ invite your best friend over? *(3 points)*
   c) ❑ throw a big party? *(5 points)*

Your score: ________

The two girls skated slowly over to the stall, where lots of people were standing around. Many of them were from different schools or the local sixth form college, but Nina and Holly recognized some pupils from their own school. There was quite a long queue, because the warm summer evening had obviously encouraged a lot of people to eat and drink outdoors. Holly and Nina joined the back of the queue, behind a group of girls from their year at school. The girls were too busy with their own conversation to even look behind them. They were discussing their plans for the rest of the summer.

local	örtlich
sixth form college	weiterführende Schule
queue	(Warte-)Schlange
to mock	lästern

"So, I'm going to get some really cool clothes when I go down to London," boasted Charlotte, who was wearing pink hot pants.

"She needs some new clothes," whispered Holly to Nina. Nina tried to laugh quietly.

"Well, I've heard that Newcastle is good for shopping, too," said Aimee. Holly started to mock about Aimee's comment, because she was still mad at her for stealing Joe from her at the ball.

Nina continued to listen to Aimee's and Charlotte's conversation.
"Why are you going to Newcastle?" asked Charlotte.
"Oh, just to visit a friend," replied Aimee casually.
Nina couldn't listen to this conversation any longer. Even though they had almost reached the front of the queue, she skated away. Holly followed her.
"What's wrong?" asked Holly.
"It's her... I know it is!" said Nina.
They stopped and sat on the floor.
"Who is who?" gasped Holly.
"It's Aimee... now it all makes sense. She's going to Newcastle to visit Marcus," sobbed Nina.
"I remember him paying her a compliment in the past... he was nice to her at my party... that's probably whom he was meeting when I was in Germany..."
"Nina, I think you're probably imagining things," said Holly.
"No, no... I'm sure. Maybe, that's why he was also in a bad mood at the ball... he was probably jealous that Aimee was dancing with Joe and that he was stuck with me."
"Now you're being silly, let's just change the subject... I can tell you about my holiday if you want..." said Holly.
Nina was furious. She just knew that she was right! She didn't want to hear about Holly's holiday, where she probably had a crush on a barman or something. She took her skates off and walked across to the empty factory. Her mind was racing. As she walked around the outside of the mill, she noticed an entrance door which was open. She had always

to gasp	keuchen, schnaufen
to pay sb. a compliment	jmd. ein Kompliment machen
Her mind was racing.	Ihre Gedanken überschlugen sich.

been intrigued about these huge buildings. She stepped inside. To the left was a huge empty space. To the right there was another door to a smaller room. She jumped when she heard a noise coming from that room. Nervously, she glanced around the door. She was not prepared for what she saw: It was Emily and Liam! They were too busy kissing to notice her. After Emily's reaction to Liam at the ball, Nina was shocked. Obviously, she had changed her mind. Nina quietly stepped out of the room and walked out of the factory with a smile on her face. If only Emily's parents could see their daughter now!

"Niiiiiiina!"

Nina looked around to see who was calling her name. She could have guessed without having to look, because it was her only friend with a voice loud enough to be heard over loud music.

"What do you want, Evie?" shouted Nina.

The girls moved closer to each other.

"What were you doing over there?" asked Evie.

"Nothing," replied Nina.

She didn't feel like telling Evie the story about Aimee, and she thought it wouldn't be fair on Emily to tell Evie what she had just seen in the factory.

"Get your skates on! The DJ has just announced that he is going to play the last song," said Evie.

Nina quickly fastened her skates and they joined a big group of people from their year, who all held hands while they skated around excitedly. At the end, Evie's dad had arrived and offered to give Nina a lift home.
In the car, Nina thought about how glad she was to have such a good group of friends. She had certainly had a better time at the rink tonight than if she had stayed in her room. It would have been a perfect evening, had it not been for Marcus and Aimee.

ÜBUNG 22: Roller disco: Bringe die Sätze in die richtige Reihenfolge!

a) Nina tells Holly that she thinks Marcus cheated on her with Aimee.
b) Aimee tells Charlotte that she is planning to visit Newcastle.
c) Nina sees Emily and Liam kissing.
d) Evie and Holly skate over to the hotdog stall.
e) Evie calls Nina over.
f) Nina gets angry and skates away from the stall.
g) Nina walks over to the empty mill.
h) Nina and Evie go home.

1	2	3	4	5	6	7	8
d							

to fasten	zumachen, anschnallen
girly	für Mädchen
to switch off	ausschalten
to get over sth.	über etw. hinweg-kommen
advice	Rat

Nina knew that she would miss Evie, who was due to go on holiday for two weeks with her parents. She also felt that she had to apologize to Holly, so she decided to invite Evie, Holly and Emily to come to her house the following evening. Nina's parents had ordered pizzas for the girls, which they ate in the lounge in front of the TV. The girls started to watch a girly DVD but got bored after a few minutes. Holly wanted to carry on watching it, but Nina switched it off because she simply couldn't stop talking about Marcus. The other girls tried to comfort her by telling her their own stories of heartbreak.

"I really thought something would happen between me and Joe... I mean, I know it's a different situation, but for a few days, I was really upset..." said Holly.

"It's not at all the same, Holly," Nina said grumpily.

"Well, I'm just saying that it usually takes time to get over such a break-up," said Holly.

"You have obviously just read that in a magazine... you have no idea!" said Nina angrily. She didn't think that her friend's advice was relevant to her at all.

"I agree with Holly... it was the same with me and Liam... he was so upset that he left the ball, but now he seems fine... it just takes time," said Emily.

When she remembered what she had seen the night before, Nina smiled. She didn't want to mention it, because she knew that it would embarrass Emily.

Evie was feeling a bit bored. She didn't really have any stories of heartbreak to add to the conversation, so she started to look through a pile of magazines. She found the girly magazines about make-up and clothes completely boring, so she began to flick through a German music magazine she picked up off the floor. She was mainly looking at the pictures because she didn't understand many of the words. Suddenly, she spotted a note and a telephone number next to an advert for The Specialheads, a group who Evie knew were due to come to the nearby city in a few weeks. Recently, Evie and Nina had travelled together to the city, to see their first real concert and they had had a fantastic time.

"You didn't invite me to this," Evie said.

Nina looked over and was puzzled for a moment. She didn't remember writing anything in the magazine.

"Aah, that's the magazine Jonas gave me at the airport. That must be his phone number!" she exclaimed.

"Well... what are you waiting for?" asked Evie.

"Call him!" encouraged Holly, who had heard all about Jonas from Evie.

"Well," said Nina, as she tossed her mobile phone in her hand. She wasn't really convinced.

"On the one hand, I really like Jonas, but on the other hand, I think it's far too soon to get involved with another boy..."

pile	Stapel
recently	vor kurzem
to toss sth.	*hier:* etw. hin und her wenden
on the one hand... on the other hand...	einerseits ... andererseits ...
to get involved with sb.	etw. anfangen mit jmd.

"Go on, Nina!" encouraged Evie.

Nina remained very sceptical. It had only been two days since Marcus had broken up with her. She was still heartbroken.

"Why is it that boys are like buses? When you're waiting for one, it never comes, but when you're not waiting, one comes straight after the other?!" asked Nina.

The girls laughed.

ÜBUNG 23: Crossword. Löse das Kreuzworträtsel!

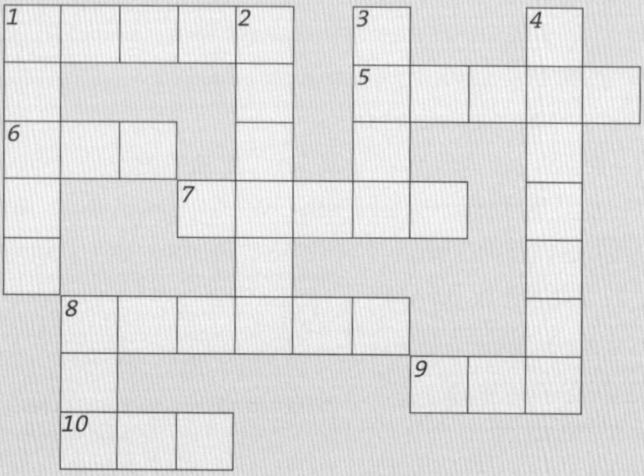

Across

1. Italian food the girls ate at Nina's house.
5. Nina gets ... when Holly talks about Joe.
6. The first number.
7. Not masculine. Evie is not very ...
8. You put it on your face, e.g. lipstick.
9. I am, you ..., he is
10. Another word for concert – the Specialheads are going to play one.

Down

1. It rings and can be mobile.
2. Help & suggestions. Nina didn't agree with Holly's ...
3. An event where you wear smart clothes and dance.
4. You find it in a magazine or newspaper.
8. A short word for magazine.

"And anyway, what if the phone number is not for me?" Nina continued weakly.
"Oh, Nina! Of course it's for you. I'm sure, I saw Jonas scribble something just before he handed you the magazine," replied Evie.
"What have you got to lose?" asked Holly.
Emily joined in, too: "Yeah, what's the worst thing that could happen?"
"Well..." said Nina slowly.
"I'm pretty sure I heard on the radio that the concert is sold out... Jonas probably has tickets... I know what I'd do," said Evie persuasively.

to scribble	hinkritzeln
persuasively	überzeugend, eindringlich
to wrestle sth. from sb.'s hand	jmd. etw. mühsam entwenden

"Evie, I'm not you," said Nina.
"It will be an amazing gig," said Evie.
"Well, why don't you call him then?" asked Nina.
Evie walked over to where Nina was sitting.
"Okay, I will..." said Evie, diving for the magazine. She tried to wrestle the phone from Nina's hand.
"Okay, okay! That's enough! I'll do it. But I'm going into another room to call him, otherwise you'll make me laugh," said Nina.
She was feeling both excited and nervous.

Nina left the room. Her hands were actually shaking. She still wasn't sure if it was the best thing to do. The other girls moved quietly towards the door and tried to listen to and watch Nina through the keyhole.

"Hello?" said a low voice on the other end of the line.

"Jonas?" asked Nina.

"That's me. This isn't Nina, is it?" asked Jonas.

"Good guess!" laughed Nina.

"I was hoping you'd call. I was wondering how long I should wait until I offered my spare ticket to someone else," Jonas said casually.

"So, you do want me to come to the Specialheads gig with you?" asked Nina. She felt as if she was dreaming.

"Unless you have other plans..."

"No... well... no! That would be absolutely amazing!" said Nina. Then a thought occurred to her.

"How did you know that I like them?" she asked.

"Well, I'm pretty observant," he said.

After a moment, she realized: "You must have seen the badge on my bag!"

to shake	*hier:* zittern
keyhole	Schlüsselloch
spare	*hier:* übrig, überschüssig
observant	aufmerksam, wachsam
badge	Abzeichen, Aufnäher

"Yup," he replied and continued, "I hope you don't think I'm some kind of crazy stranger you meet at an airport!"

"Of course not," she replied happily.

"Okay, well, I'm going camping for ten days and then there will only be a couple of days to wait. So see you there! I'll be in touch," said Jonas enthusiastically.

"Yes, I can't wait. Bye," said Nina.

As she finished the call, the other girls quickly moved back to their seats. Nina was really excited that she was going to see her favourite band, but at the back of her mind she also couldn't stop thinking about Marcus. She wished that she could travel back in time. He had been more important to her than any concert.

ÜBUNG 24: Fill in the blanks. Setze die folgenden Wörter an der richtigen Stelle ein!

plans *laughed* *voice* *wondering* *offered*

ticket *gig* *amazing* *dreaming* *asked*

1. "Hello?" said a low ....
   "Jonas?" asked Nina.
2. "That's me. This isn't Nina, is it?" .... Jonas.
3. "Good guess!" .... Nina.
4. "I was hoping you'd call. I was .... how long I should wait until I .... my spare .... to someone else," Jonas said casually.
5. "So you do want me to come to the Specialheads .... with you?" asked Nina.
   She felt as if she was ....
6. "Unless you have other ....,"
   said Jonas.
7. "No... well... no! That would be absolutely ....!" said Nina.

5

Exciting Events

5

Nun ist Nina doch froh, dass sie Jonas angerufen hat. Und natürlich freut sie sich auf das Konzert! Trotzdem wird sie den quälenden Gedanken nicht los, dass zwischen Marcus und Aimee etwas gelaufen ist.
Sie versucht sich mit einer Shoppingtour abzulenken. Ein neues Outfit für das Konzert muss her, und die Songtexte will sie auch noch alle lernen ...
Als es endlich soweit ist, ist Nina richtig nervös. Aber das Konzert ist toll, und mit Jonas versteht sie sich auch wieder blendend.
Am nächsten Tag bekommt sie dann eine Nachricht von Marcus, der sie nun doch nach Newcastle einlädt – jetzt muss Nina sich entscheiden!

Nina spent a lot of time thinking about the phone call with Jonas. She was glad that the girls had convinced her to phone him. Without her friends, she almost certainly would not have had the courage. She couldn't wait for the day of the concert to arrive. It certainly gave her something to look forward to.

To begin with, she was happy that she had some time before she would meet Jonas again, but after a few days, she wished that the holidays would pass by faster. With

Evie and some of her other friends on holiday, Emily at work almost full-time in the bookshop and planning her holiday in Florida, she found it difficult to think of activities to fill her days.

One day, she decided to meet Holly and Joe in the centre of town. Joe had just returned from his holiday and was feeling quite bored because his best friend Marcus had just moved away. Nina, Holly and Joe met in a coffee shop to have a large hot chocolate with cream. They sat on a big comfy sofa, watched the passers-by through the window and ended up having quite a long and meaningful conversation. First, they gossiped about Emily and Liam. Joe had seen them walking along the street holding hands, so he was sure that they were now boyfriend and girlfriend. Holly was happy for them, but Nina had other things on her mind. After a few minutes, the subject of the conversation changed to Marcus.

full-time	ganztags
ϟ comfy (comfortable)	bequem

"I just really miss him," said Nina.

"He has only been gone for a couple of days!" joked Holly.

"You know what I mean though... we spent so much time together and we really have always had a good time... I just feel so lonely without him," said Nina. She couldn't believe that she was talking about her feelings in front of Joe. They were good friends, but until today, Nina had seen Joe as someone she could laugh and joke around with, but whom she would never tell anything serious.

ÜBUNG 25: Quiz: Which type of guy would you be most suited to? Kreuze an, was auf dich zutrifft!

1. What colour hair do you prefer?
   a) ❑ brown
   b) ❑ blonde

2. Would you prefer him to...
   a) ❑ play the guitar?
   b) ❑ like the same bands and enjoy going to gigs?

3. Regarding school, would you prefer him to...
   a) ❑ joke around and not do much work?
   b) ❑ enjoy history and always do his work?

4. For a date, would you rather...
   a) ❑ go to the cinema, or go to the park to chat?
   b) ❑ do something different, like go to a gig?

5. Do you like it when boys show their emotions?
   a) ❑ No, they should be manly.
   b) ❑ Yes, I think they should show their emotions.

"It's so bad that I almost wish that we were back at school again... at least that would take my mind off things," continued Nina.

"You won't be saying that when we're back at school... you'll wish you could have lie-ins and relax every day," said Holly.

"I know what you mean, Nina," said Joe. "We spend the whole year wishing that the holidays were here and now that they are, we're bored and wish we were back at school. It's funny, really."

"It's rubbish," said Nina miserably. She had her good days and her bad days and today wasn't a good one.

"I'm going to miss Marcus being around at school... Now I won't have anyone to mess around with during lessons," said Joe.

Suddenly, Nina and Holly began to see Joe in a completely different light. People normally saw him as the joker of the class, but now the two girls could see his more emotional and sensitive side.

"I suppose for me that's actually a good thing... I couldn't stand it if I had to see Marcus every day and he wasn't speaking to me... At least, there is a bit of distance between us now," said Nina.

"Hmmm," agreed Holly, as she slurped her hot chocolate.

"Joe... if I told you something, would you promise not to tell Marcus?" Nina asked apprehensively.

"Of course... I'm good at keeping secrets," replied Joe.

"I'm really annoyed with Marcus for dumping me so suddenly, but there's something which upsets me much more."

"What's that?" asked Joe.

to have a lie-in	ausschlafen
joker of the class	Klassenclown
to cannot stand sth.	etw. nicht ertragen können
to slurp	schlürfen
apprehensively	besorgt, ängstlich
to keep a secret	ein Geheimnis bewahren

"Well, I'm pretty sure that he dumped me for that cow Aimee," explained Nina angrily. "You can be honest with me if you know about it, too."
"I honestly have no idea what you're talking about..." said Joe.
"See, Nina? That's what I told you!" interrupted Holly.
"I know that he really liked her..." Nina burst out. "I have no idea why... and then I heard her say that she was going to go to Newcastle to see a friend..."
"Nina, you're talking rubbish... Aimee is not a bad girl and Marcus certainly wouldn't have cheated on you," insisted Joe.
"You're just saying that because you're his best friend and, judging from what happened at the ball, you obviously like her, too," replied Nina.
"I can't believe you are trying to get me to confirm your wild imagination... you're just weird!" exclaimed Joe.
Even though Holly was still a little doubtful about Joe after how he behaved at the ball, she did believe him. She didn't

think he had anything to hide. Nina didn't say anything. Holly tried to change the subject of the conversation, but the atmosphere was so awkward that they soon ended up leaving the coffee shop to go their separate ways.

See?	Siehst du?
to cheat on sb.	*hier:* fremdgehen, jmd. betrügen
judging from...	nach ... zu urteilen
weird	schräg, seltsam
to go one's separate ways	seiner eigenen Wege gehen

For the next few days, Nina's thoughts were mixed. What if Joe and Holly were right? She would feel stupid and would have to apologize. But she was sure that she was right and couldn't get thoughts about Marcus out of her head. Then a couple of days later, she received a text from Jonas.

Can't w8 2 get out of this rain & c u.
Only a wk 2 go, hope ur ready 4 it.
Jonas xx

ÜBUNG 26: Text language. Schreibe Jonas' SMS in Standardenglisch auf!

....

....

....

....

one's mind wanders	mit den Gedanken abschweifen
belt	Gürtel
to get rid of sth.	sich von etw. befreien, etw. loswerden
excess	überschüssig
to contain	zurückhalten

After this, she couldn't stop her mind from wandering and thinking about Jonas, which felt much better than thinking about Marcus and Aimee. Jonas had something really intriguing about him. Usually, she would think it was really strange that someone she had only spoken to for ten minutes invited her to a gig. However, this seemed completely natural. She was really excited about the concert, but the text message had reminded her that she wasn't ready.

She dragged her little sister Katja into town to go shopping. She already had the first two albums by the Specialheads, but now she wanted to buy their latest album. She knew that Jonas would already have it and she didn't want to look stupid if she didn't know all of the words of the songs.

Then, she spent hours going round the shops to look for the perfect outfit. She finally bought a pair of skinny black jeans, a cool new belt and a black and red striped T-shirt.

After a couple more days, even Katja knew all of the words of the songs on the new album. Nina hardly left the house, but got rid of her excess energy by dancing around her room to the music of the Specialheads. She was looking forward to the concert so much that she could hardly contain her excitement. She managed to reassure herself that she would simply have a great time with Jonas at the concert. This didn't mean it was a date. She didn't want a boyfriend anyway. If he was *really* awful, then she would just enjoy watching the band, go home afterwards and never see him again.

ÜBUNG 27: Articles. Setze, wenn nötig, a oder the ein!

1. Nina would normally think it was unusual for a stranger to invite her to .... gig.
2. Nina owned .... first two albums already.
3. Nina was glad that she got out of .... bed to go to the disco.
4. Nina's friends thought that it was .... time to make a decision.
5. She wanted to have .... great time with Jonas at .... Specialheads concert.

Finally, it was the day of the concert. In the morning, Nina slept in, knowing that she would be out until late in the evening. She had a long bath and put her outfit on hours before she was due to travel into town. Then she sat around the house, nervously watching the clock. Four hours to go... three hours... two hours... it was time to call Evie.

"Evie, I'm scared, I no longer think I should go and meet him," said Nina.

"You, scared?! You'll be fine," reassured Evie.

"What if he tries to kiss me? I don't want to give him the wrong impression," said a worried Nina.

"Well, then don't kiss him back... just enjoy yourself," said Evie.

"What if he tries to kidnap me? He might be a complete weirdo!"

"Now you're just being stupid. You watch too much TV. He seemed like a really nice guy to me, now go and have a great time," said Evie.

"Hmm, okay... how's your holiday going?" asked Nina.

"Well, I'll tell you all about it when I get back!" replied Evie.

"Okay, thanks for your good advice, as usual!" said Nina.

"Well, that's what friends are for... off to an evening game of Frisbee on the beach now... see ya!" said Evie before finishing the call.

Nina got on the train to the city, which took around 45 minutes. She was excited because she hardly ever went into the city centre. Sometimes, she went to look around boring shops with her parents. A lot of her friends weren't allowed to go into the city centre on their own.

She was due to meet Jonas at the train station at seven o'clock. She paced up and down the platform waiting for him to arrive. It was then that she realized that she knew almost nothing about Jonas. She had no idea what train he would arrive on, or exactly where he lived. What would she do if he didn't turn up? How long would she wait? If he didn't arrive soon, they would be late for the gig. The minutes seemed like hours. Finally, at 7.15 she saw a tall blonde boy power walking towards her.

"Sorry I'm late, my train was delayed... sheep on the line," he gasped.

"Don't worry, I'm just glad you turned up," laughed Nina.

ϟ weirdo	Verrückter, Spinner
to pace up and down	auf und ab gehen
to power walk	schnell laufen
delayed	verspätet
line	*hier:* Bahngleise
venue	Veranstaltungsort
to thump	dröhnen

"You look really nice," he said.

"Thanks," replied Nina, suddenly embarrassed. It occurred to her that Marcus had hardly ever commented on her appearance.

Jonas led the way to the concert venue and Nina tried to keep up with him. Finally, they arrived there and joined the queue outside. It seemed to be taking forever to reach the end of the queue. After a couple of minutes standing there, they heard the sound of a bass thumping through the building.

"Oh no, we're missing them!" exclaimed Nina.

The queue went down and finally they got into the old theatre where the gig was held. Jonas had been there before, but Nina was amazed at the venue she had not been to before. There was a huge space downstairs in front of the stage for people to stand and then two tiers of seats above.

ÜBUNG 28: Positive sentences. Bilde unverneinte Sätze!

1. Nina didn't sleep in.

Nina slept in.

2. Nina didn't doubt that she would meet Jonas.

....

3. She didn't think he might be a weirdo.

....

4. Nina didn't get the train to the city.

....

5. Jonas didn't compliment Nina on her looks.

....

6. It turned out that Nina disliked Jonas.

....

"Phew, it's only the support band," said Jonas as they got closer.

"Let's get nearer to the stage while we can!" exclaimed Nina excitedly.

tier	Sitzreihe
support band	Vorgruppe
to cheer	jubeln
anticipation	Erwartung, Vorfreude
banner	Spruchband, Fahne

The two of them walked through the crowd. There were groups of young teenage girls, some even with their parents, but there were also quite a few couples and older people, too. The support band were pretty bad, so many people had gone to the bar or the back of the theatre, which left plenty of space for Jonas and Nina to reach the front of the venue. Everyone cheered as soon as the support band had finished and everyone in the crowd could feel the excitement and anticipation. Many of them seemed to be really big Specialheads fans and some even wore band T-shirts and held banners. Gradually, the room got more crowded. When The Specialheads finally came on stage, the atmosphere was electric.

"I'm so glad you invited me," said Nina to Jonas.

"Wonder if they'll start with 'Electric Shock'? That's my favourite song," said Jonas, just as they played the opening of 'Time Machine'.

"Doesn't look like it, but this is my favourite!" shouted Nina as the singer sung his first line.

The two of them sung along loudly and waved their arms in the air. Nina would never have imagined that she could get the chance to come so close to her favourite band.

This was the best moment of her holiday so far, possibly even of the whole year.
The Specialheads then sung hit after hit. Nina's voice was getting croaky from singing so loudly. Her ears were ringing like mad, but she didn't care.
"You look like you've been learning the lyrics by heart!" shouted Jonas.
Nina laughed and carried on shouting the words to her favourite songs. She had never had so much fun with Marcus, she thought. As the singer sang the opening line of 'This Could Be My Last Day', the crowd behind them started to go mad. A large bald guy with lots of tattoos on his arms started to push into them from behind, forcing them forwards. Nina couldn't stop herself falling against Jonas, who was trying his hardest to stop being pushed into the guy in front of him.

The whole crowd was now going mad. This was a completely new experience for Nina, but Jonas was sure to protect her. He put his arm round her shoulder and said: "Don't worry... we can move a bit further back, if you want." He then guided Nina away from the bald man and led her further back, where the crowd was a bit less packed together. "Sorry about that... I just couldn't stand being that squashed... I could hardly breathe!" explained Nina. She was a bit worried that Jonas might think that she was completely pathetic.

"Don't worry, I think we've got a better view from back here anyway... and it's not quite so hot and sweaty," said Jonas.

Nina admired the way he always made her feel comfortable. As 'This Could Be My Last Day' came to an end, Nina felt a hand on her shoulder. She turned around to find that it was Aimee from school. Now she wished she had stayed at the front. She didn't want her evening to be ruined by anything or anyone.

croaky	heiser
to learn sth. by heart	etw. auswendig lernen
lyrics	*hier:* Songtext
bald	glatzköpfig
to force	*hier:* abdrängen
squashed	zerquetscht
sweaty	stickig
to feel comfortable	sich wohlfühlen

"Is this your new boyfriend then, Nina?" asked Aimee.

Nina immediately felt awkward.

"This is Jonas... a friend," she explained. "Jonas, that's Aimee."

"Hi, nice to meet you," said Jonas politely.

"Good gig, isn't it?" asked Aimee.

Nina and Jonas nodded in agreement.

ÜBUNG 29: Prepositions. Unterstreiche jeweils die richtige Präposition!

1. They tried to get closer to/on/at the stage.
2. There was a fantastic atmosphere when The Specialheads came on/in/over the stage.
3. Nina and Jonas waved their arms on/in/about the air.
4. The crowd for/behind/between them went mad.
5. Jonas guided Nina away to/at/from the bald man.
6. They had a great time at/about/for the gig.

"I didn't think you'd be into The Specialheads," said Aimee to Nina.

"Yeah, they're one of my favourite bands... probably even my all-time favourite after tonight," said Nina as the singer thanked the audience for coming.

"Then you're a lot cooler than I thought!" exclaimed Aimee, who was dressed in a short skirt, as usual.

Nina tried to turn round to catch the end of the show, but Aimee kept talking.

"How would you fancy meeting them?" she asked.

"Meeting who?" asked Nina.

"I thought you were brainy... the band, stupid!" replied Aimee. She pointed to a tall man standing next to the stage.

"That's Rick, he is a sound engineer... He'll be able to get us all backstage access after the gig if you fancy it?" asked Aimee.
Rick gave a small shy wave.
"That's what boyfriends are for, right?" said Aimee. This comment made Nina so happy that she immediately exclaimed: "Oh yes, I'd love to meet them!"
She had been wrong about Marcus and Aimee. Aimee was probably going to Newcastle to see Rick! Nina smiled and turned towards the stage, as the band played the opening of 'Electric Shock'.
"Phew, I thought they were never going to play it," said Jonas.
The whole crowd went wild as the band played their number one hit.

After the gig, Aimee introduced Nina and Jonas to Rick, who led them through a maze of corridors which ended behind the stage. They hung around for a while in a small room full of journalists and photographers. Then the band came out wiping their heads with towels. Nina couldn't believe she was standing just inches from her favourite band. Johnny, the lead singer, didn't

audience	Publikum
to catch sth.	*hier:* etw. mitbekommen
ϟ to fancy sth.	auf etw. Lust haben
brainy	gescheit, clever
backstage access	Zugang hinter die Bühne
maze	Labyrinth

seem interested in the press. He waved away the photographers and went to chat to a group of teenage girls, who had won backstage passes in a radio competition. He signed some posters for them and then walked over to where Nina and Jonas were standing.

to wave sb. away	jmd. wegschicken
cute	süß, niedlich
couple	Pärchen
ϟ awesome	großartig, fantastisch
to keep up with sb.	mit jmd. mithalten
to bend down	sich bücken, sich runterbeugen
passionate	leidenschaftlich
to squeeze	sich zwängen, quetschen

"So..., cute couple..., did you guys enjoy the gig?" asked Johnny.

Nina could feel herself turning red. Everybody just seemed to assume that she was going out with Jonas!

"Um... yeah... it was awesome," said Nina.

"Yeah, we were right at the front... I was so glad that you played 'Electric Shock'," continued Jonas.

"Well, that's my favourite song to sing, so we left it until last," said Johnny.

He continued to chat to them as if he really cared about their opinions, which seemed unusual for someone so famous.

Suddenly, Jonas looked at his watch: 11.20 p.m.

Nina's last train home was at half past eleven!

"Come on, Nina, we've gotta go and get our trains," said Jonas.

They quickly said thanks and goodbye to Johnny, Rick and Aimee, before running out of the building and

towards the station. Jonas seemed pretty athletic while Nina struggled to keep up with him. They finally reached the station at 11.29. The train was already there.

“Well, thanks for inviting me, it’s been an amazing evening,” gasped Nina.

“Thanks for coming,” replied Jonas calmly as he bent down to give Nina a kiss on the lips.

It wasn’t a long or passionate kiss but it gave Nina butterflies in her stomach. She didn’t have time to react because the train doors shut and she had to run to squeeze in quickly. The train pulled away. On the journey home, she couldn’t stop thinking about that kiss. Did it mean anything? Did he want to see her again? He certainly hadn’t mentioned anything about that.

ÜBUNG 30: Reading comprehension. Beantworte die folgenden Fragen zur Geschichte!

1. Why did Nina's opinion about Aimee change?

....

2. What irresistible offer did Aimee make Nina and Jonas?

....

3. What kind of people were in the room behind the stage?

....

4. Why was Jonas shocked when he looked at his watch?

....

The next day, Nina felt completely shattered. She woke up and looked at her phone. It was already midday! She had an unread text message, so, still half asleep, she read it.

> Hi babe hope ur ok. Missing u. Flat big enough for a visitor if u want 2 come and stay? Love Marcus xx

This was a big surprise to Nina. At first she thought that she was dreaming. It was strange, but during the previous day she had almost totally forgotten that Marcus existed! She briefly contemplated going to visit him in Newcastle, especially as she now knew she was wrong about Aimee. However, after a while, she texted him back to tell him that she thought that they had now gone their own ways, as he originally wanted, and that it would be a bad idea for her to visit.

shattered	zerschlagen, erschöpft
briefly	kurz
to contemplate	in Betracht ziehen

She thought about how strange her decision was, because only last week she would have done anything to get a text like this from Marcus. She would have been so happy and gone to visit him as soon as possible. She couldn't help but think that Jonas had something to do with the fact that her feelings had changed. She didn't hear from Marcus again after her reply.

Later that day, Jonas called her to check that she had got home okay the night before. They chatted for about an hour and arranged to meet in the city the following week. Nina was extremely happy. She hadn't wanted to get into a new relationship, but was happy with the way things were going with Jonas. They weren't boyfriend and girlfriend but they just got on together really well. She couldn't wait to see him again. It had certainly been a mixed summer so far, but she could feel that it was just beginning to get better!

Lösungen und Glossar

Lösungen

ÜBUNG 1:

1. liked, yellow 2. England, year 3. happy, cheered Nina up 4. often, close 5. Evie, Nina, RE

ÜBUNG 2:

1. bored 2. gorgeous 3. sarcastically 4. want 5. half an hour 6. pass by 7. conversation 8. think 9. exam 10. choice

ÜBUNG 3:

Mostly a): You are a creative type of person, a bit like Holly. Sometimes you get into trouble because you dream during lessons. However, there's nothing wrong with dreaming about a creative career.

Mostly b): You are an intellectual type of person, a bit like Emily. You always do well in exams and you have definite plans for a successful future.

Mostly c): You are a sporty type of person, a bit like Evie. You are always full of energy and sometimes find it difficult to sit still during lessons at school.

Mostly d): You don't care, a bit like Marcus. You have never really liked school and often risk getting into trouble with the teachers.

A mixture: You like variety, a bit like Nina. You don't really mind school, you like to hang around with your friends and you enjoy trying out new things.

ÜBUNG 4:

1. I wasn't 2. She'd like 3. They've planned 4. You're 5. They'll go 6. I'm hoping 7. I haven't seen 8. She's been

ÜBUNG 5:

1. falsch 2. falsch 3. richtig 4. falsch 5. richtig 6. richtig 7. falsch 8. falsch

ÜBUNG 6:

1. They give her a lot of money.
2. She commented on the house and Nina's appearance.
3. It was warm and sunny.
4. She was worried that they might ruin her party.
5. He only came to ask Emily to the ball.
6. She thought that he was shy and awkward.

ÜBUNG 7:

1. handbag, shoulder bag, plastic bag
2. textbook, storybook, picture book
3. girlfriend, boyfriend, best friend
4. football, netball, summer ball

ÜBUNG 8:

Mostly a): You are a fun-loving dancer. You enjoy to get dressed up and to dance with your friends, but you don't need to be treated like a celebrity.

Mostly b): You are the star of the ball. You spend the whole year planning your outfit and date, and the summer ball is your favourite day of the year. You love to be treated like a celebrity.

Mostly c): You are a bit of a tomboy. You only go to a ball if your friends want you to be there. However, you feel quite uncomfortable to be the centre of attention, and you wouldn't make a good celebrity!

ÜBUNG 9:

1. b 2. c 3. b 4. c

ÜBUNG 10:

1. frasch (fresh) 2. anoying (annoying) 3. laffed (laughed)
4. liest (least) 5. disskusting (disgusting) 6. tung (tongue)
7. woarning (warning) 8. expleyned (explained)

ÜBUNG 11:

1. smart – casual 2. beautiful – ugly 3. excited – bored
4. lad – girl 5. laugh – cry 6. clean – filthy 7. sad – happy

ÜBUNG 12:

1. c 2. d 3. b 4. a

ÜBUNG 13:

1. find 2. pronounce 3. get along 4. predicted
5. refused

ÜBUNG 14:

1. I just couldn't sleep at all last night.
2. This is the first time someone in my form has won the award for the best results in their year.
3. There's no use in running away.
4. I've got nothing to stay here for, I'm a complete failure.
5. At least we've got our little holiday to look forward to.

ÜBUNG 15:

1. reassure 2. tomorrow 3. mind 4. decision 5. boyfriend
6. holidays 7. parents 8. Staying

ÜBUNG 16:

1. It was Jonas who said that he had been to the castle many times before.
2. It was Evie who said that she could imagine living in Germany.
3. It was Jonas who told Nina that she looked as if she was on a different planet.
4. It was Nina's excuse for not listening that she was sleepy.
5. It was Evie who told the others that it was time for the flight.
6. It was Jonas who offered to lend Nina a magazine.

ÜBUNG 17:

B	S	A	P	Y	E	A	H	U	G
A	O	C	O	H	O	P	M	S	I
R	K	Y	P	S	D	U	M	P	R
G	E	C	F	U	G	L	H	O	L
U	G	N	L	R	K	O	P	G	F
M	A	A	S	C	I	V	J	A	R
E	E	F	B	I	S	E	S	L	I
N	T	I	N	E	S	J	N	S	E
T	A	E	H	C	T	I	O	D	N
M	D	U	Q	X	B	D	G	F	D

ÜBUNG 18:

1. b 2. c 3. b 4. a 5. c

ÜBUNG 19:

1. delighted 2. neighbour 3. slippers 4. noisy 5. break
6. push

ÜBUNG 20:

1. more bored 2. best 3. larger 4. largest 5. warmest
6. surprised 7. more surprised 8. more determined
9. most determined 10. friendlier

ÜBUNG 21:

3-6 points: You are definitely a good girl. You almost always follow the rules and wouldn't let your friends and family down. You should be proud of yourself!

7-10 points: You are not a bad girl. You sometimes follow the rules, but you can be influenced by others or by the chance of rewards for yourself.

11-15 points: You are probably a naughty girl. Well, rules are made to be broken, aren't they? Your parents can't even trust you to stay in the house on your own and you don't really appear to have any morals yet.

ÜBUNG 22:

1. d 2. b 3. f 4. a 5. g 6. c 7. e 8. h

ÜBUNG 23:

1 P	I	Z	Z	2 A		3 B			4 A	
H				D		5 A	N	G	R	Y
6 O	N	E		V		L			T	
N			7 G	I	R	L	Y		I	
E				C					C	
	8 M	A	K	E	U	P			L	
	A						9 A	R	E	
	10 G	I	G							

ÜBUNG 24:

1. voice 2. asked 3. laughed 4. wondering, offered, ticket 5. gig, dreaming 6. plans 7. amazing

ÜBUNG 25:

Mostly a): You are suited to Marcus. You would have a good time with him and you would spend a lot of time together. Be warned though, he is always in trouble at school and he also doesn't really talk about his emotions.

Mostly b): You are suited to Jonas. You would go to gigs or exhibitions together and also have intellectual conversations with him. However, sometimes he can be quite direct.

ÜBUNG 26:

Can't wait to get out of this rain and see you. Only a week to go, hope you're ready for it. Jonas xx

ÜBUNG 27:

1. a 2. the 3. – 4. – 5. a, the

ÜBUNG 28:

1. Nina slept in.
2. Nina doubted that she would meet Jonas.
3. She thought he might be a weirdo.
4. Nina got the train to the city.
5. Jonas complimented Nina on her looks.
6. It turned out that Nina liked Jonas.

ÜBUNG 29:

1. to 2. on 3. in 4. behind 5. from 6. at

ÜBUNG 30:

1. It changed when she found out that Aimee already had a boyfriend.
2. She offered backstage passes to Nina and Jonas.
3. There were photographers, journalists and competition winners.
4. Jonas was shocked because it was nearly time for Nina's last train.

Glossar

a bit of a	ein(e) ziemliche(r)
ϟ to ace sth.	etw. mit links schaffen
actually	tatsächlich, eigentlich
advice	Rat
to aim at sth.	es auf etw. anlegen
anticipation	Erwartung, Vorfreude
to apologize	sich entschuldigen
apprehensively	besorgt, ängstlich
to approach	nahen, bevorstehen, sich nähern
associated with	zusammenhängend mit
to assure	versichern
at such short notice	so kurzfristig
audience	Publikum
ϟ awesome	großartig, fantastisch
awkward	unbeholfen
backstage access	Zugang hinter die Bühne
badge	Abzeichen, Aufnäher
bald	glatzköpfig
banner	Spruchband, Fahne
to be about to	im Begriff sein zu
beauty contest	Schönheitswettbewerb
to be desperate to do sth.	verzweifelt versuchen, etw. zu tun
to be due to do sth.	etw. tun sollen
behaviour	Verhalten, Benehmen
to be hit by reality	von der Realität eingeholt werden
to be in touch	in Verbindung sein, sich melden
belt	Gürtel
to bend (bent, bent) down	sich bücken, sich runterbeugen
ϟ to be sick of sth.	von etw. die Nase voll haben
to be (was, been) stuck	festsitzen
to be (was, been) unlike sb.	ungewöhnlich für jmd. sein, nicht zu jmd. passen
black bags underneath one's eyes	dunkle Ringe unter den Augen
to blare out	herausschmettern
bleached blonde	wasserstoffblond

ϟ bloke	Typ, Mann
to blow (blew, blown) one's nose	sich die Nase putzen
to board	einsteigen, an Bord gehen
ϟ to bop about	herumhüpfen
bow	Schleife
bow tie	Fliege
brainy	gescheit, clever
to break (broke, broken) up with sb.	mit jmd. Schluss machen
briefly	kurz
to bring sth. to life	etw. sehr anschaulich erklären
briskly	flott, rasch, zügig
to brush up	auffrischen
ϟ to bug sb.	*hier:* jmd. nerven
to bump into sb.	mit jmd. zusammenstoßen
to burst into tears	in Tränen ausbrechen
butterflies in one's stomach	Schmetterlinge im Bauch
by now	inzwischen, mittlerweile
to cannot stand sth.	etw. nicht ertragen können
carousel	*hier:* Gepäckband
to carry on	fortfahren, weitermachen
to catch a glimpse of sb.	jmd. flüchtig sehen
to catch (caught, caught) sth.	*hier:* etw. mitbekommen
caught up in one's thoughts	in Gedanken vertieft
celebrity	Prominente(r)
to change the subject	das Thema wechseln
to chat	plaudern
to cheat on sb.	*hier:* fremdgehen, jmd. betrügen
cheeky	frech
to cheer	jubeln
to clash	nicht harmonisieren, sich beißen (Farben)
to clear away	abräumen
to clench sth.	etw. umklammern, festhalten
ϟ clever clogs	Schlaukopf
college	höhere Schule
to come (came, come) up	*hier:* drankommen
ϟ comfy (comfortable)	bequem
concealer	Abdeckstift
concerned	beunruhigt, betroffen
concrete floor	Betonboden
confident	selbstsicher
consequently	folglich, als Folge
to contain	zurückhalten
to contemplate	in Betracht ziehen

couple	Pärchen
to cram in	hineinpacken
croaky	heiser
to cross off	durchstreichen, wegstreichen
to curl up into a ball	sich zusammenrollen, sich einigeln
curly	lockig
customer	Kunde
cute	süß, niedlich
daring	mutig, waghalsig
to dash	rasen
date	*hier:* Begleiter(in)
deaf	taub
to deal with sth.	mit etw. klarkommen
delayed	verspätet
delighted	hocherfreut, begeistert
departures board	*hier:* Abflugtafel
derelict	baufällig, herrenlos
despite	trotz
determined	entschlossen
devastated	am Boden zerstört
dimples	Grübchen
disgusting	ekelhaft, widerlich
disused	ausgedient, stillgelegt
dot	Punkt
dotted	verstreut
to doubt sth.	etw. bezweifeln
to drag	ziehen, zerren
to dread sth.	jmd. graut vor etw.
to drop sth.	etw. fallen lassen
due	fällig
ϟ to dump sb.	mit jmd. Schluss machen
edge	Seite, Rand, Ecke
effort	Anstrengung, Einsatz
embarrassed	verlegen
encouragingly	aufmunternd
envelope	Umschlag
eventful	ereignisreich
eventually	schließlich, letztendlich
excess	überschüssig
exhausted	ausgepowert, erschöpft
expression	Gesichtsausdruck
to face sth.	sich einer Sache stellen
factory	Fabrik
to fail	scheitern, durchfallen
failure	Versager(in), Misserfolg

faint	leise, schwach
ϟ to fancy sth.	auf etw. Lust haben
to fasten	zumachen, anschnallen
to feel (felt, felt) comfortable	sich wohlfühlen
to feel like doing sth.	Lust haben, etw. zu tun
to feel the need	das Bedürfnis haben
filthy	schmutzig, verdreckt
to flick through	durchblättern, überfliegen
flowery	geblümt
flustered	nervös, aufgelöst
to fly (flew, flown) by	verfliegen, im Flug vergehen
to force	*hier:* abdrängen
form	Klasse
frilly	aufgeputzt
full-time	ganztags
to gain marks	Punkte bekommen (Leistungsbewertung)
to gasp	keuchen, schnaufen
ϟ geeky brain-box boy	seltsamer Strebertyp
to get an early night	früh zu Bett gehen
to get (got, got) at sb.	mit jmd. streiten, jmd. auf die Nerven gehen
to get divorced	sich scheiden lassen
to get into the swing of things	in Schwung kommen, sich auf etw. einlassen
to get involved with sb.	etw. anfangen mit jmd.
to get on well	gut (miteinander) auskommen
to get over sth.	über etw. hinwegkommen
to get rid of sth.	sich von etw. befreien, etw. loswerden
girly	für Mädchen
to give sb. a hug	jmd. umarmen
ϟ Good riddance!	*hier:* Ein Glück, dass wir die los sind!
to go one's separate ways	seiner eigenen Wege gehen
gorgeous	großartig, umwerfend
gossip	Klatsch, Tratsch
gradually	allmählich
gravel driveway	Kiesauffahrt
to ground sb.	jmd. Hausarrest erteilen
grumpily	mürrisch
ϟ gutted	am Boden zerstört
handsome	gutaussehend
ϟ to hang (hung, hung) around	herumhängen
to hang up	auflegen

ϟ to have a crush on sb.	in jmd. verknallt sein
to have a lie-in	ausschlafen
to have eyes in the back of one's head	Augen wie ein Luchs haben
to help oneself	sich bedienen
Her mind was racing.	Ihre Gedanken überschlugen sich.
hibernation	Winterschlaf
high-powered	anspruchsvoll
Hinduism	Hinduismus
to hire	mieten
ϟ to hit the dance floor	abtanzen, die Tanzfläche stürmen
host	Gastgeber(in)
to hug	umarmen
in a rush	in Eile
inch	Zoll (brit. Längenmaß: 2,54 cm)
inquisitive	wissbegierig
intriguing	faszinierend
jealous	eifersüchtig
to join in	sich beteiligen
joker of the class	Klassenclown
judging from...	nach … zu urteilen
to keep (kept, kept) a secret	ein Geheimnis bewahren
to keep up with sb.	mit jmd. mithalten
keyhole	Schlüsselloch
knee-length	knielang
lack of	Mangel an
ϟ lad	Junge
lap	*hier:* Runde
to learn sth. by heart	den Text auswendig lernen
to lend (lent, lent)	leihen
liberal-minded	tolerant, liberal
life and soul	*hier:* Mittelpunkt
ϟ like chalk and cheese	verschieden wie Tag und Nacht
like-minded	gleichgesinnt, auf gleicher Wellenlänge
line	*hier:* Bahngleise
to link arms with sb.	jmd. unterhaken
local	örtlich
long-distance relationship	Fernbeziehung
luggage area	Gepäckbereich, Gepäckabholung
lyrics	*hier:* Songtext
to make a friend for life	eine(n) Freund(in) fürs Leben gewinnen
to make a reference to	*hier:* verweisen auf

to make up for sth.	etw. wieder gutmachen, ausgleichen
mark	(Schul-)Note
to match	zusammenpassen
maze	Labyrinth
mess	Chaos
mind-reader	Gedankenleser(in)
to mind	etw. dagegen haben
mirror	Spiegel
miserably	unglücklich
to miss out on sth.	etw. verpassen, sich etw. entgehen lassen
to moan	jammern, sich beschweren
mobile	*hier:* Handy
to mock	lästern
mood	Stimmung
to mope around the house	zu Hause sitzen und Trübsal blasen
to mutter	murmeln
necklace	Halskette
to nickname sb.	jmd. einen Spitznamen geben
to nod	nicken
not everybody's scene	*hier:* nicht jedermanns Sache
observant	aufmerksam, wachsam
obviously	offensichtlich
occasion	Gelegenheit
occasionally	gelegentlich
to occur to sb.	jmd. in den Sinn kommen
on the one hand ... on the other hand ...	einerseits … andererseits …
one's mind wanders	mit den Gedanken abschweifen
opportunity	Gelegenheit
out of the corner of one's eye	aus dem Augenwinkel
over-hyped	übertrieben, aufgeblasen
overweight	übergewichtig
owl-like	eulenhaft
to pace up and down	auf und ab gehen
to panic about sth.	wegen etw. in Panik geraten
participant	Teilnehmer(in)
ϟ party animal	Partylöwe
passer-by	Passant(in)
passionate	leidenschaftlich
to pat sb. on the shoulder	jmd. auf die Schulter klopfen
to pay sb. a compliment	jmd. ein Kompliment machen
persuasively	überzeugend, eindringlich
to pick sb. up	jmd. abholen

pickled cabbage	Sauerkraut
pile	Stapel
place	*hier:* Haus, Wohnung
poetry	Gedichte, Poesie
politely	höflich
possibly	möglicherweise
to pour one's heart out	sein Herz ausschütten
to power walk	schnell laufen
to predict sth.	etw. voraussagen, prophezeien
prepared	vorbereitet
progress	Fortschritt
to pull away from sb.	sich jmd. entziehen, ausweichen
to pull oneself together	sich zusammenreißen
puzzled	verwirrt
queue	(Warte-)Schlange
to raise one's hand	*hier:* aufzeigen, sich melden
rather	ziemlich
RE (religious education)	Religion(sunterricht)
to reassure	versichern
recently	vor kurzem
register	Klassenbuch
to relate to	zuordnen, beziehen auf
relieved	erleichtert
reluctantly	widerstrebend
resort	Ferienort
to retake (retook, retaken) exams	Prüfungen/Klassenarbeiten wiederholen
retakes	Nachprüfungen
revelation	Enthüllung
rink	*hier:* Rollschuhbahn
to rub	reiben
to run a club	eine Arbeitsgruppe leiten
rye bread	Roggenbrot
sane	ausgewogen, vernünftig
scenery	Landschaft
to scream and shout at sb.	*hier:* sich anbrüllen, streiten
to scribble	hinkritzeln
secret admirer	heimliche(r) Verehrer(in)
secretly	insgeheim
See?	Siehst du?
selfish	egoistisch
session	*hier:* Unterrichtsstunde
to shake (shook, shaken)	*hier:* zittern
shakily	wackelig
shame	Schande, Jammer

shattered	zerschlagen, erschöpft
shiny	glänzend
to shriek with delight	vor Freude schreien, kreischen
to sigh	seufzen
silky	seidig
sixth form college	weiterführende Schule
skinny	spindeldürr
ϟ to skive off school	blaumachen
to slide (slid, slid)	schieben, gleiten lassen
slightly	etwas, leicht
to slurp	schlürfen
sniffle	Schniefen
to snigger	kichern
to sob	schluchzen
sociable	gesellig
social skills	soziale Kompetenzen
sore	gereizt
spare	*hier:* übrig, überschüssig
sparkly	funkelnd
speech	Vortrag
speechless	sprachlos
ϟ Spill the beans!	Spuck's aus!
to spin (span, spun) around	herumwirbeln
spot	*hier:* Pickel
squashed	zerquetscht
to squeeze	sich zwängen, quetschen
stack	Stapel
stage	Bühne
stall	Stand
to stand up for oneself	sich behaupten
to stare at	anstarren
to stare into space	ins Leere starren
to stay the night	über Nacht bleiben
stocky	stämmig
ϟ street cred(ibility)	Glaubwürdigkeit (überzeugendes Auftreten)
to stroke	streicheln
to struggle	Mühe haben
studious	fleißig, lernbegierig
stunning	umwerfend
suitable	passend
suited	mit einem (Herren-)Anzug bekleidet
support band	Vorgruppe
to sway from side to side	sich hin und her wiegen
sweaty	stickig

to switch off	ausschalten
sympathetic	mitfühlend
to take one's mind off sth.	nicht mehr an etw. denken, sich ablenken
ϟ to talk rubbish	Blödsinn/Müll reden
talkative	gesprächig
to tease	sticheln, sich lustig machen
to text sb.	jmd. eine SMS senden
ϟ the more, the merrier	je mehr, desto besser
throat	Hals, Rachen
ϟ throw (threw, thrown) a party	eine Party schmeißen
to thump	dröhnen
tier	Sitzreihe
tiny	winzig
to begin with	anfangs
toddler	Kleinkind
tomboy	Wildfang
tongue	Zunge
toothpaste smile	Zahnpastalächeln
to toss sth.	*hier:* etw. hin und her wenden
to treat sb. differently	jmd. anders behandeln
to tune back in	*hier:* sich wieder konzentrieren
to turn up	auftauchen, erscheinen
uncomfortable	unbequem
unique	einzigartig
unnecessary	unnötig
unprompted	spontan
(it is) up to sb.	jmd. überlassen sein, von jmd. abhängen
venue	Veranstaltungsort
voicemail	Anrufbeantworter
waistcoat	Weste
warning glance	warnender Blick
waste bin	Mülleimer
to wave sb. away	jmd. wegschicken
weird	schräg, seltsam
ϟ weirdo	Verrückter, Spinner
well-thumbed	zerlesen
to wipe	(weg)wischen
to wrestle sth. from sb.'s hand	jmd. etw. mühsam entwenden
to yawn	gähnen
You scared the life out of me!	Du hast mich zu Tode erschreckt!